P9-DGC-916

Managing to Be Free

Managing to Be Free

A Practical Guide to Organizing Home Priorities

Shirley Daniels
Marian Jones Clark

BAKER BOOK HOUSE
Grand Rapids, Michigan 49516

Copyright 1987 by
Agape Ministries

ISBN: 0-8010-2973-2

Second printing, December 1987

Printed in the United States of America

The personal illustrations used in this book are taken from real-life situations. However, names have been changed.

Unless otherwise identified, Scripture quotations are from the New American Standard Bible, © The Lockman Foundation 1960, 1962, 1963, 1968, 1971, 1972, 1973, 1975.

Scripture quotations identified AMP are from the Amplified Bible, © 1965 by Zondervan Publishing House.

Scripture quotations identified NIV are from the New International Version, © 1978 by New York International Bible Society.

Scripture quotations identified LB are taken from The Living Bible, © 1971 by Tyndale House.

Paraphrase of 1 Corinthians 13 from *Taste and See* by Margaret Wise, published by Moody Press.

Comments on Paul from "Scheduling for Saints" by Charles E. Stanley, *In Touch* magazine, 1984.

Comments on quiet time from *Meditative Prayer* by Richard D. Foster, InterVarsity Press, Downers Grove, Illinois.

Definition of a 'family' from *What Is a Family?* by Edith Schaeffer, Fleming H. Revell Company, Old Tappan, New Jersey.

Quotation from *Eighth Day of Creation* by Elizabeth O'Conner, published by Word, Inc., Waco, Texas.

Do You Know? is from a tract by Jerry R. White Jr., published by Agape Ministries, Titusville, Florida.

"The Beatitudes of a Christian Wife" is something I had clipped from a magazine years ago and don't know the name of the magazine nor the year. It was anonymous.

Contents

The Beatitudes of a Christian Wife

Author Unknown

Blessed is she whose daily tasks are a labor of love, for willing hands and a happy heart translate beauty into a privilege, and her labor becomes a service to God and to those she loves.

Blessed is she who opens the door to welcome both stranger and well-loved friend, for gracious hospitality is a test of true Christianity and spiritual stewardship.

Blessed is she who mends stockings and toys and broken hearts, for her understanding is a balm to those in need.

Blessed is she who scours and scrubs. She knows that cleanliness is important, but that forgiveness of sin in the human heart can only be purified through the blood of Jesus Christ.

Blessed is she whom children love, for the love of a child is more to be valued than fame and fortune.

Blessed is she who sings at her work, for music lightens the heaviest load and brightens the dullest chore.

Blessed is she who dusts away doubt and fear, and sweeps out the cobwebs of confusion, for her faith in Christ will triumph over all adversity, and her patience of hope will be rewarded by the Lord.

Blessed is she who serves laughter and smiles with every meal, for her buoyancy of spirit is an aid to mental and physical digestion. The Bible says, "A merry heart doeth good like a medicine."

Blessed is she who preserves the sanctity of the Christian home, for hers is a sacred trust that crowns her with dignity and results in her children arising and calling her blessed, and her husband praising her also.

1

Introducing Renae

It was Renae's birthday, and she was thirty-nine. *Old,* she thought. *I'm getting old.*

She stood on the porch, looking out into the quiet street beyond the screening, and blinked back the tears. Hers was a pretty street, with homes set on groomed lawns. Palm branches and orange-laden trees seemed to dance in the morning haze.

It promised to be another hot Florida day: the cicadas were humming loudly already. But here on the porch it was cool and dark, almost as dark as early this morning, when Steve had left on a business trip, flinging angry words back at her: "Would it be too much to ask to have a clean shirt with buttons on it ready for me? Just *one* shirt?"

Her husband had broken into her hesitant apology with "Forget it! I suppose I should be used to it after fifteen years. I'll just pick up a couple at the airport."

"When will you be back, Steve?" she called to his stiff retreating back.

He had answered, "Maybe Sunday," and slammed the door.

She shrugged in defeat. That's the way it was now. She and Steve weren't talking much anymore; they didn't seem to have anything important to say to each other.

Domino batted a soft paw at a page of yesterday's newspaper, strewn untidily over the floor. Renae glanced around at the tiny black and white kitten. How messy the patio looked! The clutter seemed to reflect the state of her life.

Why was there never enough time? She needed to pick up the empty glasses that still sat where they had been left last night. Melissa's good sweater was all scrunched up in the corner. And that stack of letters was still waiting to be answered.

She could almost imagine the pile of dirty dishes staring at her back from the sink. Her mind whirled as she remembered the hamper running over with clothes. Steve was right: there *were* several shirts missing buttons—oh! and Kathy's jeans, too, on the sewing machine, waiting to be fixed. And she had to get off that hospital committee. Why had they asked her anyway? There, under one edge of the newspaper, was Melissa's sneaker, for which they had searched high and low before bus-time. (She'd had to take an old outgrown pair to school this morning.)

Dust and confusion were everywhere. What were the magic words that would make it all disappear?

Renae began crying weakly. She was busy all day—every day—and yet she was not getting the basics done around the house. The two girls were not much help either. They were always going someplace, doing something, studying for some special assignment.

That's the way it is when you get into the teens, she reminded herself. Melissa wasn't really a teen, of course; although, at twelve and a half, she was already displaying the same irresponsible traits as Kathy. The thought made her stomach convulse. How could she be a good mother if she couldn't even get her own act together?

The doorbells chimed. Automatically she glanced at her watch—she loved its sweet gold face; it had been her fifteenth anniversary gift from Steve.

Betty! she thought. *I promised I would go with her to that—that dumb class! At church, yet!*

"Coming," she called.

As always, Betty looked immaculate. This morning she was wearing a black-and-white-striped linen blazer, a slim black skirt, and a red tailored shirt. Even her earrings matched: bold black outlined in gold.

I wish I had mended the blouse that matches my rose skirt, Renae thought. She looked enviously at Betty's red and white spectator pumps; her own espadrilles seemed dull and uninspiring.

"Let's hurry," Betty said with a grin. "We want to be there right on time."

2

Setting Your Priorities

Renae looked around curiously as she and Betty took their seats. She was surprised to see so many women. Some looked great in color-coordinated outfits; others, like herself, were carelessly put together. She didn't like to be classed with the dowdy ones (even in her own mind) and decided that next time—if there was a next time!—she would look as good as anyone there.

She crossed her bare tan legs and wondered why she had come. She caught a glimpse of the wife of the Ford dealer in town. *Funny that she's here,* Renae mused. The memory of her own dirty, cluttered house popped into her mind and made her tired just thinking about it. Sudden laughter brought her attention back to the chairwoman, who was introducing the speaker.

"This morning I want you to meet Shirley Daniels, the wife of our minister of counseling. Shirley's a busy homemaker and mother of two. She spends a lot of time in ministry to others, yet she has ample time for her husband and

14

children. *She's planned it that way!* Pick one word to describe this little dynamo of energy and you'd probably say 'organized.' In fact, she's so organized even her canned goods are arranged according to color!"

Renae leaned over to Betty and whispered, "I don't like her already."

"Give her a chance," Betty chuckled.

The coordinator looked down at her notes and continued. "Shirley keeps her beautiful home neat and clean; she has disciplined herself to clean house certain hours of certain days each week. She even makes up all her menus a week in advance—which saves time in the grocery store and in the kitchen. Shirley told me it wasn't always this way, however—"

"I should hope not," Renae muttered. "What is this Shirley, anyway?"

The chairwoman continued: "All went smoothly during their first seven years of married life. Shirley had no problem balancing her teaching career with helping her husband in his ministry. Then—but I'll let Shirley tell you about that."

The coordinator turned to a slender woman, who rose and came to the platform.

Renae noted approvingly Shirley's short blond haircut and her pink coral suit. *Classy!* she thought. *The hottest color this season.* Renae knew, because she had wanted to get one herself. And that bow blouse in dusty gray and pastel tones pulled it together impressively.

Shirley smiled and began: "Wow! That sounds like a super-mother, super-wife, super-housekeeper, *SUPER-WOMAN!* And that's not what I am. I'm not an expert in home management. I'm just a homemaker like you. Having been a minister's wife for some years and now the mother of two junior-highers, I've struggled as you have. Trying to be—" Here she paused, took a deep breath, and then said all at once, "—a loving mother–good wife–Sunday-school teacher–discipleship leader–daughter to my parents–daughter-in-law to my husband's parents–sister–neighbor–friend—and oh! all of those responsibilities we have."

She gulped, then went on. "Sometimes we get to the point where we wonder how we can get any balance in our daily lives. It's all coming in on us. We don't quite know which way to go first. And we sometimes feel like failures."

Soft groans and audible sighs through the audience showed that Shirley had touched a sore point. Renae whispered to Betty, "She doesn't know the half of it!"

"A lady asked me as I came in," Shirley went on, "how long it took me to learn what I'm going to share today. And I said, 'Would you believe eighteen years?'

"'Well, then there's hope for me!' she answered. There is hope—for all of us."

Renae studied the women in front of her, wondering if anyone else felt as hopeless as she did.

"Something I heard during the 1980 Presidential campaign made a lot of sense," Shirley continued. "Senator Barry Goldwater said, 'If you don't know where you're going, any road will take you there.' This is also true in our personal lives. If we don't know where we want to go as women, we can't possibly end up where we want to be!

"What about *your* life? What is your life purpose? Twenty years from now when you look back, what do you want to have accomplished? What are your goals for this year?"

Renae thought, *Goals, huh? I've never even thought about goals for a housewife. My life is a whirlwind, with things to do swirling higher and higher.*

Shirley went on, "Think first with me about purpose, priorities, and goals and how they relate to your management of time. For me, *priorities* are the steering wheel and *time management* the tires of the vehicle to get me where I want to go. Priorities keep me on the highway of my purpose in life."

Shirley's voice faded in and out of Renae's mind. She still wasn't convinced, as she thought about herself and her family, but Shirley was continuing.

"I've found I cannot have order in my home if I don't have order within myself. You see, order first comes inside us and then is expressed without. So we're going to talk about personal organization first. And that includes your personal priorities and your own schedule."

The room was electric with attention. But Renae felt like standing up and saying, "Look, I've tried it all—and for some people, like me, *nothing* works!"

The perky speaker seemed unaware of Renae's skepticism. "Some time ago, I took a little time test. Frankly, I was surprised at what I found out about myself. It really made me think! I'd like us all to take it right now. At the end of each row you'll find a bunch of papers stapled together. Please take one set for yourself and then pass the rest along to the others in your row. If you need a pencil, hold up your hand and one of my helpers will give you one."

The Test of Time

1. Do you ever get the feeling that there just aren't enough hours in a day?
   A. No   B. Occasionally   C. All the time

2. How many terrific things happened to you last month?
   A. At least five   B. One or two   C. None

3. How often are you right on time for things?
   A. Always   B. At least half   C. Practically never
                         the time

4. Did you ever catch yourself just "puttering around"?
   A. No, never   B. Sometimes   C. A lot

5. Think of the New Year's resolutions you made last January. Have you accomplished any of them yet?
   A. Yes!   B. No   C. Resolutions? I haven't
                                                made any in years!

6. How would you describe your day so far?
   A. Productive   B. Fairly productive   C. Disastrous

Everything seemed to move efficiently. As Renae looked
down at her "Test of Time," Shirley said, "Now, please circle
one of the answers under each question."

Renae, knowing she was in trouble, found that she was
circling every *C*.

"The test was simple, wasn't it?" asked Shirley. "Now
score yourself. For each *A* answer you circled, give yourself
one point; for each *B* answer, two points; for each *C* answer,
three points. Total your score." Shirley waited a moment and
then went on. "If you scored seven or more points, you're not
managing time as effectively as you might."

Renae wondered, *Maybe that is my problem!*

"We are all busy people," Shirley said. "We have no trouble filling up the hours! I often look back over a week and ask
myself just what was accomplished as far as my goals and
purposes are concerned.

"Would you all please look at the page after your time
test?" (See p. 18.) There was a rustling of paper. "Up at the
top, you can see 'My Life Purpose: What I Hope to Be.' Then
there's a little space and you'll find next 'My Priorities' and
under that, numbers from one to five."

"I'm not going to ask you to write down your thoughts
now, but could you? And if you could, are you living your
daily life according to your priorities and purpose?"

Renae looked around at the others, wondering how many
could do it. She almost missed Shirley's next words.

"Remember the story of the farmer who had a target on
his barn and always hit the bull's-eye? When a friend asked
him how he did it, the farmer answered, 'Oh, it's easy! I shoot
first and then I draw the bull's-eye!'"

The women laughed as Shirley continued. "Too often
that's what we homemakers do. We fool ourselves into
thinking that whatever happens is what we had targeted for
the day. In reality, there is no bull's-eye—we are just drifting.

"One of the great New Testament writers knew about
bull's-eyes. He wrote in First Corinthians 9:26, 'Therefore, I
run in such a way, as not without aim. . . .'"

My Life Purpose: What I Hope to Be

_____

_____

_____

_____

_____

_____

_____

My Priorities

1. _____

_____

2. _____

_____

3. _____

_____

4. _____

_____

5. _____

_____

_____

_____

How to Develop a "Bull's-Eye"

1. Build it from the Word of God.

2. Write it out.

3. Work over it. Pray over it.

4. Make It **comprehensive, but specific**—not just "to please God," but asking **how** God wants me to please him specifically in my life.

"If you're like me, it's not enough just to say, 'I need a life goal.' My big question is, '*How* do I go about developing a bull's-eye—a life purpose?'"

The room echoed with agreement. "That's right." "That's what I need." "Tell us, Shirley." And Renae added to herself, *Make it simple and make it clear!*

"Possibly it would be helpful to make suggestions on how to do it and then illustrate by explaining how *I* did it. I don't want to linger too long on this, but it is the basic principle on which all management of our home priorities rests. I found four steps that helped me and they are outlined on your next sheet of paper."

Shirley continued: "To illustrate—my own life purpose is to abide in continuous fellowship with my heavenly Father in order that I can share his desires, burdens, and life. I base this on Philippians 3:10: 'That I may know Him, and the power of His resurrection. . . .' This is exciting! His life is my life. His desires will become more important than my own!

"One of my friends, Linda, has recognized her basic target as being to love God. She wants to become all that God wants her to be as a woman, wife, and mother. That's a wonderful life purpose, but it has to be broken down into practical steps, called priorities and goals.

"I went to the Scriptures to find out what, if anything, it might have to say about priorities. Matthew 22:37 and 38 gave me the answer. Jesus said that you shall ' "love the Lord your God with all your heart, and with all your soul and with all your mind." This is the first and greatest commandment' [NIV].

"So, *that* has to be my first purpose and my first priority. In order to love God, I must have the assurance that I know Jesus Christ as my Lord and Savior. He is the Prince of Peace. Without him, I would not even expect to have peace, only turmoil. 'There is no peace for the wicked,' says the Lord in Isaiah 48:22.

"So I would suggest to any of you who do not know Christ that you invite him into your life. I would be glad to help you do that after we finish." (See Appendix A for the Way-of-Salvation pledge and an introduction to the Good News.)

"King David said in Psalm 5:3: 'In the morning, O LORD, Thou wilt hear my voice; In the morning I will order my prayer to Thee and eagerly watch." This means that I take my best time of day, usually early morning, for being alone with God. Every day I worship him and receive his love and guidance. He prepares my heart for the events of the day before they begin to crowd in on me.

"But what about you young women—who are sure, as Joyce Landorf says, that 'you will be *forever* knee-deep in diapers, formula and fatigue'? When is *your* best time?

"I have a young friend with two babies under three who felt terribly guilty about this. 'So tell me,' she asked angrily, 'when—just *when*—do I fulfill my first priority?' Her eyes filled with tears as she continued, 'Is it when I've been up all night with the baby and he cries again at four-thirty or five? Am I supposed to have a quick time with the Lord before I go to my child? By that time, he'll have wakened Diannah and I'll have *two* crying babies!'

" 'Of course not!' I replied. 'The Lord who gave you the babies—and remember, they are a gift from the Lord, according to Psalm 127:3—knows you have to care for them. God

made those babies with their special needs, and he made
you, too.' The Scripture that will comfort your heart, as it did
mine on more than one occasion, is found in Isaiah 40:11,
which tells us that the Lord 'will gently lead the nursing
ewes.' *Gently,* it says. *Gently.*"

All over the audience, tired-eyed mothers sighed and
seemed to relax a little.

"The Lord knows your heart. This is your opportunity to
do what Brother Lawrence suggests: to practice the presence
of God in everything. Maybe, in another session, we will be
able to go into this a bit more fully, but for now, examine your
heart.

"If it is so, tell God that you love him and want to spend
time with him. Then ask him to show you when that time is
to be. He will. I can guarantee it. Do you think the Creator of
the universe can't show you how to be creative in your life in
meeting him who loves you so much?

"Remember, too, that *best* is different for different people,
it can vary for each of us even during our life. I appreciate
what Dr. Richard Foster, associate professor of theology and
writer in residence at Friends University in Kansas, says in
answer to 'What time?'

> The answer to that varies from person to person and often
> is different for any individual at different points in his or her
> life. For example, in my high-school years the morning hour
> was especially valuable; as a college student a free hour just
> before lunch met my needs better; in graduate school less
> frequent but more extended periods were most helpful; and
> in more recent years the morning time again seems best. You
> will find your own rhythm. Find the time when your energy
> level is at its peak and give that, the best of your day, to Him.

"Remember, I said a while ago that *priorities* are the steering wheel of my life vehicle and keep me on the highway of
my purpose in life. Because of this, I need to have my priorities firmly in my mind and heart so I can make daily
scheduling decisions based on them.

"For instance, the other day I needed to wash clothes, go to a food-preservation demonstration, attend a luncheon-planning meeting, finish preparing a message for the next day, and be sure I was at home when the children got back from school. What to do with all these activities pulling at me? I know you've felt like that, too.

"Well, I sat down to study and make some notes—and had three phone calls between nine and nine-thirty. That wasn't too bad, except I was in the study, and the phone is in the bedroom, so I had to run all the way down the hall to answer the phone each time. After the third time, when I sat down at the desk again, I prayed, 'Lord, will you protect my time?'

"My prayer was interrupted—the phone rang again and I raced down the hall again. This time it was the school saying Debbie was not feeling well and I would have to pick her up. My first thought was, 'Why today, Lord? You know I've got all this washing to do and this message to finish!'

"The Lord answered me right back, asking. 'Who's more important: Debbie or your message?'

"I found my answer very quickly, 'Debbie!' So I said, 'Thank you, Lord' and went to get my daughter.

"She wasn't really sick, just not feeling too perky. I put her to bed, threw the first load in the washer, and went back to the study to work on my message, after calling to excuse myself from the planning luncheon. In two hours Debbie woke up hungry and ready to go back to school.

"God was helping me get my priorities right, because the interruptions didn't even disturb me. See, it really *is* children before housework and church work.

"One dictionary definition of 'priority' is 'being first in rank, time or place; having first claim.' We all know that trying to be all these different women—to do all these things—can be overwhelming. But Ecclesiastes 3:1 says, 'There is an appointed time for everything. . . .' Therefore, I should have time to do everything God wants me to do. Right? So God will never overload or overwhelm me. Right?

It's up to me, then—to you and to me—to discover which responsibility comes first.

"Establishing priorities is essentially a matter of making choices about the use of time. Barbara Walters says, 'Women have to balance their time better than men because they don't have wives.'

"Now I want to hurry on and give you the rest of my list of priorities and the Bible verses they're based on. You don't need to try to copy all this down. The papers you can pick up at the door as you leave will have these Scriptures listed, so you can look them up yourself at home. One is "Scripture Priorities,' and the other is 'Shirley Daniels' Life Purpose and Priorities.'

"My foremost purpose for life and my first priority is loving and serving God.

"My second priority is based on something God said in the Garden of Eden. It is found in Genesis 2:24: 'For this cause a man shall leave his father and his mother, and shall cleave to his wife; and they shall become one flesh.'

"If I'm to become 'one flesh' with my husband, that means there are some adjustments I'm going to have to make. I must get to know well not only God, but my husband, too. And I'll want to relate to Danny the way God designed me to. Oneness should characterize our marital relationship. I am to complete him; he is to complete me. This takes time.

"One way Danny and I make this kind of time to be together is reserving Friday nights for each other. Also, after supper every evening, we share our day with each other while the children are out playing. My commitment to Danny is to take priority over *all other* human relationships."

Suddenly Renae said to herself, *There are parts of what she's saying that rather make sense. I'd like to spend more time with Steve.*

Shirley's voice claimed Renae's attention again: "Then there's my third priority—the children. Where, in your time priority, do your children rate? We all know that when they are infants and toddlers, they seem to be first all the time, almost to the exclusion of everything and everybody else! Then, as they grow up, our days get filled with busyness. Don't you find that? Sometimes the children get pushed aside for other people and other things. So we get caught in the middle of trying to give our offspring enough time, yet not letting them take over our lives completely.

"We must remember that children have been entrusted to us by God to mold for him. Our goal in child rearing is godliness.

"Another priority is our living parents. We need to remember that God says in his commandments and in Ephesians 6:2 to honor them. How can we honor our parents? Well, if they live in the same town, we can spend time with them. If they are away, we can write or phone regularly. Their needs should be our next priority after husband and children." Shirley paused here for emphasis. When every eye was looking her way, she continued, "And we can ask our parents for counsel.

"My next priority is home, based on Proverbs 31:27. The 'excellent woman,' whom we'll be talking about later, 'looks well to the ways of her household, and does not eat the bread of idleness.'"

Renae sighed and leaned toward Betty to mutter, "All this reminds me of a bionic woman!"

As if she had read Renae's mind, Shirley added: "If this already seems more than enough, let me assure you that housework is a *job*, not a burden. And, like any other job, there is a right way to do it: a quick and efficient way. There are also many hard, inefficient, and slow ways. To be effective in the role of homemaker, we have to plan creatively and then learn to be flexible! More about this, next session.

"God—my husband—the children—our two sets of parents—our home! At this point, you may feel like the little girl who was so afraid of being left out after her brother arrived that in any new situation she would wail, 'But what about *me?*'

"I had to work through this question, too. What *about* me? We need private time: personal grooming, looking after clothes, reading and hobbies, friendship, and proper rest. Where do these things fit in? Although private time may seem like a luxury as you look at the time requirements in your life, a certain amount of solitude is necessary for everyone.

"Remember, Jesus told us, 'Love your neighbor as *yourself.*' Obviously, that presupposes that you love yourself. Do you? If you *are* happy with the way you are, don't allow anyone to tell you that you are not happy or cause you to dwell on your shortcomings. It is a true joy and possible for anyone to walk closely with the Lord and have an inner peace with him by your side.

"God says that you are redeemed, sanctified, a saint, and precious in his sight. If you or I focus on our own shortcomings, we can't love ourselves. If we can't love ourselves, we can't love others.

"Do you realize that God and you, God and I, are in partnership? He does his part and I do mine. My part is to present the best *me* possible. The self I present is part of what people see of God. That's why my spiritual nourishment and growth are important. That's why my health matters and my mind is important. And how I look has a bearing on the impressions people have of God, too. I have to have self-respect, and even love for myself, in order to present my Partner—God—in the best light.

"Do you remember the story about the mother of John Wesley? She had twelve children. When she needed private time to pray or meditate, she would sit on a chair in her kitchen and put her apron up over her head. That meant that she was not to be disturbed!"

Renae had picked up the word *twelve* and thought, *With twelve children, I'd be stark raving mad.*

"Last on my priority list are my outside activities, my ministry—those things I do with and for my church, my neighbors, and my community."

Scripture Priorities

"There is an appointed time for everything . . ."
Ecclesiastes 3:1

1. Lord (personal devotions)	Matthew 22:37, 38
2. Family	
a. husband	Genesis 2:24; Proverbs 12:4
b. children	Psalm 127:3
c. other family members	Ephesians 6:2
3. Homemaking	Proverbs 31:27
a. housekeeping duties	
b. shopping	
c. repairs	
d. errands	
e. supervising children	
4. Myself	Matthew 19:19
a. health/exercise	
b. recreation	
c. growing	
5. Others	Colossians 4:17
a. ministry	
b. church activities	
c. neighbors and community	

Note: If you are a working woman, see Colossians 3:22, 23.

Renae had had enough. It made her tired just to think of all the things Shirley had on her priority list. She told herself, *I suppose maybe there are that many things in my life, too. But I sure don't want to think of them all at once!* She switched off her mind.

The class was over with a noisy hubbub of quick hellos and good-byes, mothers rushing off to get their preschoolers from the nursery, and everybody picking up the slips with the Bible verses.

Shirley Daniels' Life Purpose and Priorities

My Life Purpose: To be in continuous fellowship with my heavenly Father in order that I may share his desires, burdens, and life.

Based on: Philippians 3:10
"That I may know Him, and the power of His resurrection."

My Priorities:

Based on: Ecclesiastes 3:1
There is an appointed time for everything . . .

1. God

Based on: Matthew 22:37, 38 (NIV)
"'You shall love the Lord your God with all your heart, and with all your soul, and with all your mind.' This is the first and greatest commandment."

First in the morning

Based on: Psalm 5:3 (NIV)
Morning by morning, O Lord, you hear my voice; morning by morning I lay my requests before you and wait in expectation.

2. My Husband

Based on: Genesis 2:24
For this cause a man shall leave his father and his mother, and shall cleave to his wife; and they shall become one flesh.

3. My Children

Based on: Psalm 127:3 (NIV)
Sons are a heritage from the Lord, children a reward from him.

Proverbs 22:6 (NIV)
Train a child in the way he should go, and when he is old he will not turn from it.

4. Our Parents

Based on: Ephesians 6:2, 3
Honor your father and mother (which is the first commandment with a promise), that it may be well with you, and that you may live long on the earth.

5. My Home
   Based on: Proverbs 31:27
                   [The godly woman] looks well to the ways of her
                   household, And does not eat the bread of idleness.

                   Psalm 127:1 (NIV)
                   Unless the Lord builds the house, its builders la-
                   bor in vain.

6. Myself
   Based on: Luke 10:27b and Matthew 9:19 paraphrased
                   "You shall love your neighbor **as yourself.**"

7. My Outside Activities, My Ministry
   Based on: 1 Peter 3:8, 9
                   To sum up, let all be harmonious, sympathetic,
                   brotherly, kindhearted, and humble in spirit; not re-
                   turning evil for evil, or insult for insult, but giving a
                   blessing instead; for you were called for the very
                   purpose that you might inherit a blessing.

"It was okay," Renae commented to Betty as they left the meeting, "but I sure don't see how this could help me. My house is still a mess and it always will be!"

"We'll be talking about that in one of our next sessions," said a soft voice behind her.

Renae turned around. It was Shirley! "Oh! I—I'm sorry," she stammered.

But Shirley said, "I think you'll find it all fits together. Don't get discouraged. You'll enjoy completing your work sheet, using the Scripture references."

"Oh, um, sure, sure," Renae mumbled, embarrassed that she had not been paying attention when Shirley gave out the homework.

"Good!" Shirley smiled. "I'll look for you next week."

3

Renae Attempts Cupboard Cleaning

The house was cool and restfully dark when Renae returned from the afternoon's shopping spree—such a contrast to the blazing heat outside! Renae thought gratefully of the relaxing bath she had promised herself and slipped her shoes off her aching feet. She tossed the three shopping bags onto the sofa.

If she went back to class next week, she wanted to be as tastefully dressed as any of the others, and the pale toast dress she had bought would be just right. The vivid red jacket and bright woven sash coordinated with it beautifully. The red shoes were a perfect match to the jacket, and she could use them with other outfits, too.

Renae put her fingers up to her throbbing temples; she could feel a headache coming on. Turning toward the hall, she stumbled over a pile of books. Drat it! She had promised Steve last week she would take them back to the library.

Now she would owe a fine. *But,* she thought, *Steve will never know.* Slyness had become a pattern of life with her, since she hated the scenes he made when she had "forgotten" something.

Deciding to close her eyes to the mess all around her, Renae headed toward the bathroom, shedding her clothes along the way. She slid into the tingly bubbles and stretched her head back, trying to relax her neck muscles. Maybe if she rotated her head, like she saw on television last week. . . . She tried it, slowly one way and then the other. Nope, no good. Nothing was any good anymore; nothing helped.

Like that dumb class this morning, she thought. She had gone along because she had refused Betty so many times. *It was a waste. Well, maybe not. That thing Shirley had said about—what was it?—oh, that a wife is supposed to "complete" her husband.* Funny to think that in order to realize his full potential in life, Steve needed her! That business about the buttonless shirts this morning still hurt! And the house *was* a mess most of the time.

God first, husband next, and then the children. That sure wasn't the way in her life! Although it had been meant to be a funny story, Renae could understand the feelings of that little girl who asked, "What about me?"

As she dried off in the luxurious turquoise towel, she thought maybe she would look up the Bible verses on that little paper Shirley had given out. If she had time. And maybe she would try to get things cleaned up a bit before Steve got back. Wouldn't he be surprised! She'd do it tonight, while the girls were away at their slumber party.

As she powdered herself, Renae said to herself, *Nah! I'm all relaxed now. I could really go to sleep. One more night won't make any difference. And when I get up I'll be all fresh and ready to go.* She yawned. *I'll work on it all tomorrow,* she vowed, as she fell into bed.

The next morning, Renae awakened early and drowsily watched through the window as the sky lightened, bit by bit. A single bird twittered, fell silent, twittered again. Renae's feet instinctively sought the reassurance of Steve's warmth beside her. She shivered again, remembering her dream, and peered at the empty pillow. Her dream taunted her: *He's not coming back. He's never coming back!*

"Of course, he's coming back. He said maybe he'd be home Sunday," she said out loud, feeling foolish as she heard her own voice in the stillness. An inner voice reminded her that he had been angry when he left, had said, "Maybe." And in view of what she had heard yesterday, she supposed he didn't have much to come home to.

Renae realized she had loved Steve for a long time and still did. Upset or not, he was hers. Of course he would come back Sunday. "Of course," she said again.

She hopped out of bed, running over in her mind all that she would do—clean closets, cupboards, and drawers. That would show him she could be organized if she wanted to. She'd show Steve, and Shirley Daniels, and Betty, and all the other ladies in that class.

Late in the afternoon, Renae was stacking towels in the linen closet when behind her a man's voice said, "Hey! This place looks like a cyclone hit it!"

"Steve! You startled me!" Renae looked around her in dismay. "This is only Saturday. I—I didn't expect you until tomorrow!"

"It looks like it!"

"I started to clean the hall closet, and I was doing great until I ran into the Monopoly game. I took it to the kids' bedroom and they wanted to know how to play it. So we played for a couple of hours. Then I realized, 'Hey, I've got to get back to the hall closet,' so I started in *again*. But I found a bunch of magazines and wanted to look through them to decide which ones to toss and which to keep, and I found a recipe I wanted to try. So that reminded me I hadn't taken the meat out of the freezer for dinner tonight. Then I went to the kitchen to get out the chops and saw some towels stacked on the counter and—and—I was just doing that when you walked in!"

"I thought you and the kids would be glad to see me back a day early!"

"Oh, Steve, I am, I am! I just wanted to get the place fixed up. And it's more of a mess than it was before," Renae wailed.

"Why don't you get dressed up and we'll all go out for supper."

"Oh, Steve! That sounds wonderful. I'll just stuff all this back into the closet. I can clean it up another time. I promise I'll do it soon. I promise. Really!"

4

Discovering the Two A's

A re you a thermostat or a thermometer?"
Shirley asked the class next week. Renae smiled, wondering
what she meant.

"Don't know?" Shirley cocked her head, reminding Renae
of a bright-eyed sparrow. But no sparrow was as pretty as
Shirley in that luscious mint-colored suit. "Well, what does
a thermometer do?" she prompted.

"Tells what the temperature is," a young woman answered from the back of the room.

"Right. A thermometer registers what heat there is. But a
thermostat regulates the heat; it *sets* the temperature in a
home. So which one are you? Do you act? Or react? In your
home, do you merely record the temperature—or do you set
the warmth yourself?"

There was a slight pause as each woman considered the
question.

"Each of us can *set* the atmosphere in our homes. Did you
ever notice—when you've been off-balance—the whole

33

household suffers? And when you've been calm and serene, isn't everyone else content? Margaret Wise wrote what I think is a beautiful paraphrase of First Corinthians 13:

> Though I provide my family with every necessity of life and have not love, I have failed as a parent.
> Though I spend most of my time working for material needs in my home and can discuss intelligently and helpfully with others how they may improve their home life,
> And though I profess absolute faith in every member of my family, if I have not love, I am nothing.
> Though I spend most of my time at home, and though I plan many excursions and picnics for my family's pleasure, and have not love, it profits me nothing.

"What do the members who live there think about your home? What is the atmosphere of your home? What do people sense when they come in and sit down in your living room? Which words would most aptly describe your home? Peace? Warmth? Cheerfulness? Love? Rest? Serenity? Laughter? Music?" Here Shirley's lilting tones changed to a more somber note. "Or anxiety, quarreling, bickering, bitterness, coldness, materialism?"

Renae had never before considered what her family might think about their home. And she didn't particularly like the way her thoughts were leading her now. She shrugged her shoulders, crossed her knees, and sighed when she remembered how bad the atmosphere had been last Wednesday night when Steve had come home late from work, tired and grumpy. She cringed, remembering her thoughtless words: "Well, I'm sorry, but I've had a hard day, too, cooped up here with these four walls and these kids of yours and I'd like a little consideration myself!" Steve had turned away and walked into the den, shoulders slumping.

Renae shook her head, as Shirley's words seemed a continuation of her own thoughts.

"*You* set the atmosphere. Let us be as Peter tells us: . . . 'the inward adorning and beauty of the hidden person of the heart, with the incorruptible and unfading charm of a gentle and peaceful spirit, which (is not anxious or wrought up, but) is very precious in the sight of God [First Peter 3:4, AMP].'

"If we have this beautiful spirit of gentleness and quietness, it will pervade our homes."

Sure, Renae grumbled, petulantly talking back to Shirley in her mind, *but how can we be gentle and quiet when it isn't our nature? It sure isn't mine!*

As if in answer to the unspoken question, Shirley went on, "Love, peace, and gentleness are spiritual qualities that only God can give, so if you don't have them, don't think it's hopeless. God can change you. I know. He's changing me."

Shirley stopped speaking and looked around the room. Then she went on slowly, "The Two A's are *atmosphere* and *attitude.* I trust each one of you will consider them this week as you go about your own home. Maybe you'll want to ask God to show you and help you change, too.

"Let me quote a book I was reading recently. John Ruskin, an English poet, wrote: 'When love and skill work together, expect a masterpiece.'

"Now picture your home as you would like it to be: clean, well organized, tasteful, and attractive. The atmosphere is warm and inviting. It is a home that honors the Lord. That is a testimony in the neighborhood. It is love's masterpiece."

Briefly Renae thought about this. A masterpiece? Well, *she* hadn't been creating any masterpieces lately. But what a vision to have for one's home! *As far as I'm concerned,* Renae grinned wryly, *my masterpiece is piling higher and higher with things to do.*

Shirley's voice pulled Renae's thoughts back: "We want a home where our Lord Jesus can come in and feel comfortable. That's where the Two A's, *atmosphere* and *attitude,* come in. Our home would also be easy to move around in, pleasing to look at, and comfortable.

"In John 11:5 we read about the home of three of Jesus' closest friends: 'Now Jesus loved Martha, and her sister, and Lazarus.' Judging by what happened in that home, I think it was equally true that Martha, Mary, and Lazarus loved Jesus. They had the kind of home to which Jesus loved to come.

"In spite of Martha's fussiness and her concern with food and meals—somebody has to be concerned with that!— there was an atmosphere that cordially welcomed the presence of the Son of God and that gave him the rest and recreation he so often needed during his ministry.

"I want that kind of home, don't you? I want everyone and everything within its walls to cry 'Welcome!' to God and the Master. I want everyone within it to be a Martha, doing every chore from washing the dishes to kneeling in God's corner, in the knowledge that they do it to prepare the house for the coming of God. I want everyone in it to be a Mary, too, ready to sit at his feet when he comes, and learn from him. I want everyone in it to be as quietly faithful, even unto death, as Lazarus was. I want a home—don't you?—in which every occupant will know that God is in it, every hour, every minute, and that *he likes to be there.*

"Let's consider for a few moments the atmosphere of our home as it relates to husband and wife, remembering that if there is tension between the two of you, if your relationship is not good, the whole family is going to be affected.

"Have you thought recently about *God's* purpose in marriage? At the very beginning, God stated his purpose for marriage in Genesis 2:24, AMP: 'Therefore, a man shall leave his father and his mother, and shall become united, and shall cleave to his wife; and they shall become one flesh.'

"What is God's purpose in my marriage? He wants to develop a spirit of oneness, of intimacy, of being open and able to share with each other. God sees us as one. In Genesis 2:23, Adam says: 'This is now bone of my bones,/And flesh of my flesh;/She shall be called Woman,/Because she was taken out of Man.'

"Notice that we women are part of our husbands, one flesh. God sees us as *one,* one in body, soul, and spirit. Many marriages are one in *body,* meaning they have a good sex relationship. But God wants us to go further. He wants us to be one in *soul*. That means there's sharing, there's communication between husband and wife, an openness, a sensitivity to each other's needs.

"And then God wants us to be one in *spirit*. That means that both partners are growing in maturity as Christians, being conformed to Christ's image. If your husband is not a Christian, this part is not possible just now. But it is what God desires for your home.

"What kind of marriage do you have? Are you just one-third married—just one in body? Or maybe you're two-thirds married. I find a lot of marriages where the partners are one in body and one in spirit, but there's a great deal of conflict in the soul area. There's a lack of communication; barriers have been erected over the years, and it just seems that they cannot get through to each other.

"Maybe one has hurt the other and the hurt one has become resentful. Or perhaps one nags and the other has become defensive. There are subjects they don't dare discuss because one or both of the partners are too sensitive. God has shown me—through personal experience—four secrets of getting your husband to talk to you.

"First, *accept* him just like he is. God told me, 'I gave Danny to you because he is what you need to make you more like my Son Jesus. He is my gift to you.' Now, *my* idea had been that my husband was pretty good, but there were a few changes that I wanted to make. And my way of going about it was to point out these few little things and then to keep reminding him about them—the word, I think, is *nagging!* So God showed me what he has to say about nagging; it's in Proverbs 25:24: 'It is better to dwell in the corner of the housetop than to share a house with a disagreeing, quarrelsome, and scolding woman [AMP].'

"Well, when I read that, I asked the Lord in tears, 'God, how do you want me to accept him?'

"And God said, 'One way you have not been accepting him is that you always compare him—unfavorably—with your father.'

"I thought for a while and realized that was true. My father was a handyman. He could repair the car. Fix a faucet or anything else in the house. Repair a tile. Make shelves and do carpentry. He could fix anything.

"But my husband wasn't designed by God to be a handyman; he was called to be a minister. However, from the beginning of our marriage, I had expected him to fix anything that went wrong. It was a terrible source of frustration for him. He'd tear a thing apart and then couldn't put it back together. Finally we talked it over calmly and decided together that it would be best to call a repairman and let Danny do what God had designed him to do: minister to people through listening and counseling.

"It helped me so much when I saw that I just needed to accept him as he was and to accept the purpose for which God had made him. I believe it was Ruth Graham who said, 'If you'll make your husband happy, God will make him good.' It's not my place to make him good, anyway. That's God's business. But I sure do enjoy making him happy!

"It's the same with a non-Christian husband. God will do the changing. When *we* try to make the changes in him, the husband has only one reaction: defensiveness. He says to himself, *She doesn't like me the way I am. Why try?* My natural tendency is to resist someone who is trying to change me, too. Why should my husband be different?

"My big mistake in this area was trying to compare people who are called to totally different roles. I'm called to be a wife and mother. It would be pretty silly if someone tried to compare me with a sky-diver, now wouldn't it?

"Second, God took me to Ephesians 5:33 and told me to *admire* my husband: '. . . the wife must see that she deeply respects and reverences her husband . . . that she defers to him, praises him, and loves and admires him exceedingly [AMP].'

"Have you done that lately? Have you thought about all the good qualities your husband possesses? You must have thought he had some pretty good qualities or you wouldn't have married him. If you haven't told him recently how wonderful he is, you might try that. And do it sincerely. This is the very opposite of criticizing him, of cutting him down to your friends, of making snide remarks at parties. And it is a great thing for breaking down defenses and barriers that have come between you.

"Think about how you can build your husband up. Criticizing him and comparing him unfavorably with others is in sharp contrast to admiring him. And sometimes it seems we can't be neutral: we either do one or the other!

"Ask God to show you your husband's good qualities. Ask him to remind you of the things you admired in the past. And then just tell your husband about them.

"The third thing God showed me was that I was to submit to my husband—meaning that I'm to *adapt* myself to his lifestyle. I used to get uptight when Danny wasn't home on time for dinner. But, in a minister's family, you just can't be that way. God showed me it was a form of rebellion in me— that I was an unsubmissive wife and needed to adapt myself to my husband's schedule.

"In short, I had to become a yes-let's-do-it rather than a no-I-don't-want-to wife. God said in the beginning, as we are told in Genesis 2:18: 'It is not good for the man to be alone; I will make him a helper suitable for him.' We are to be a suitable helper, a *helpmeet* for him, one who will meet his needs. God has given us the special place of being the emotional center of our home. He has entrusted us to meet the emotional needs of our husbands and each other member of the family.

"God created woman to complement, to complete man. We are man's intuition, his gentleness, his restraining power, his compassion. First Corinthians 11:7 tells us that 'the woman is the glory of man.'

"God's original creation is beautiful. Let's keep it that way. We are truly women, in the highest degree, when we belong to God. When we do not belong to him and do not allow him to give us guidance, things get out of focus, and there is

confusion. In this confusion we are less than we should be as
women, and we do not present the true picture of ourselves.
He made us not as the 'weaker sex,' but as the *gentler* part.
Let us cultivate the gentleness of Christ in our characters.

"The last thing God showed me, also from that Ephesians
5:33 verse, is that the wife is to praise her husband, love him,
appreciate him exceedingly. I did appreciate my husband to a
certain degree, but I hadn't let him know it.

Four Secrets of Communicating with Your Mate

1. ACCEPTING	vs.	nagging
2. ADMIRING	vs.	criticizing
3. ADAPTING	vs.	demanding my rights
4. APPRECIATING	vs.	belittling, ungratefulness

"Let the wife see that she . . .

"respects and reverences . . ."	ACCEPTS
"notices and regards . . ."	ADMIRES
"defers to him . . ."	ADAPTS
"praises, loves and admires him exceedingly . . ."	APPRECIATES

Ephesians 5:33, AMP

"You know," Shirley said with a soft smile, "before we
were married and soon after, my husband used to bring me
little gifts. Not because it was any special occasion, but
because he wanted to. We were on such a tight budget that I
began saying, 'Honey, why did you do that? You know we

can't afford it. Why flowers, when I need something to cook in?'

"I didn't mean to be ungrateful; I was being practical! But to him it sounded as though I didn't really appreciate his choice of a gift. You know what happened, don't you? He stopped bringing the little extra gifts home—until sometime much later. And, by then, I had learned a little bit more about being appreciative.

"I think you'll find, as I did, that the by-product of a loving relationship between husband and wife is a loving, peaceful, Christ-honoring atmosphere in the home. You'll find on your first paper today some secrets about communicating with your husband that I'm sure you'll find helpful.

"Last week I asked you to work on your priority sheets. Before God, you were to try to find out what your purpose in life is, what your goals are, and to establish your personal priorities. I trust you have done this; if you did, I know it was a blessing to you."

Betty smiled smugly, while Renae wondered if she looked as guilty as she felt. But Shirley was continuing to speak: "If you didn't do your homework, please don't get a guilty feeling about it. That doesn't help any of us! Just determine to get down to work and do it. That's what you are here for, isn't it? To help you establish and manage your individual home priorities.

"I read recently that *time* is the only commodity in the world all people share alike. Your homework this week won't take any particularly heavy thinking on your part, but it will require the discipline of a segment of time each day.

"You'll notice that the sheets of paper being passed out now are blank, except for the titles, although one has a grid on it. Your homework this week is for you to find out what really happens with your time.

"You need to know how you are using your time. I suggest you use a pencil, rather than a pen, and at the end of the day, write down exactly what you did that day, noting when and how much time each activity took. Fill it in on the sched-

My Present Schedule

TIME	SUNDAY	MONDAY	TUESDAY	WEDNESDAY	THURSDAY	FRIDAY	SATURDAY
6:00							
7:00							
8:00							
9:00							
10:00							
11:00							
12:00							
1:00							
2:00							

3:00	4:00	5:00	6:00	7:00	8:00	9:00	10:00	11:00	Additional Things To Do

ule—the blank grid. You may have to make notes during the day, to jog your memory. Please bring both the priority paper and the grid with you next week, so we can work together in class on a realistic schedule tailored for *you*.

"Thanks for coming again today. I trust you are taking away with you something to think about and pray about for this next week. Don't let the homework be a burden to you. Enjoy it—realizing the purpose behind it! 'Bye for now!"

Renae smiled back at Shirley and determined in her heart that *this* week she really would get the homework done.

5

Renae—And Steve's Priority Rating

Whatcha doing, honey?" Steve's voice was sleepy, as he put his hand lovingly on Renae's shoulder. Startled, she turned her head. Steve was barefoot, his green-striped pajamas rumpled. He ran a hand through his wavy auburn hair, trying to smooth down all the sticking-up ends. Renae smiled to herself. He looked just like the little boy they had always wanted and never had. "I thought you'd be coming to bed before this," he added.

Renae glanced at her watch. "Oh, I didn't realize it was after one." She started to pick up her papers, but Steve had seen something in the round circle of light on the desk that caught his interest, and he reached over for it. It was her priority sheet.

"Why, darling!" Steve's voice was light, teasing, but Renae could tell from the little muscle throbbing in his jaw that he was moved. "I had no idea I rated so high in your life. After God! Wow! Am I really that important to you?"

Renae blushed. It was one of the things about her that Steve had always loved, but it made her furious with herself. She didn't know what to say, so she just nodded her head.

Her dark brown hair was haloed in the lamplight and a soft curl cast shadows on her face. She looked vulnerable somehow, and young. Tentatively, Steve reached out his hand and put a tender finger on her cheek in the old loving way he had done when they were first married. Her eyes filled with tears. She looked up at him and whispered, "It's been so long since you've done that." They both were suddenly still, looking at each other for the space of a couple of heartbeats.

"Come." Steve's arm turned her gently toward the dark hall. "It's time for bed. What were you working on anyway?"

"Oh, it's a class I'm taking. About managing home priorities. I've been so bad at it that I'm trying to get things straightened around. Our homework this week is to make out a schedule, showing how I spend my time. But it's so hard for me," she sighed.

"Hey," he chuckled in the old way, deep down in his throat. "I can help you with that. Let *me* make out your schedule for you."

"Oh, it's not that kind of schedule. I guess that comes next. This is just what I'm doing *now.*"

Renae laid her head back on Steve's shoulder and closed her eyes. It had been a long time since they had walked like this, body warm against body, down the darkened hall. She didn't want to say anything to spoil this sweet closeness, but Shirley had said that they were to work on their schedules themselves. She sighed again and thought, *I'll finish it up someway myself tomorrow. I shouldn't have tried to do it tonight anyway, with Steve home.*

She reached her arm around him. Together they turned into the bedroom.

6

Organizing Your Schedule

Good morning!" Shirley greeted the women cheerfully.

The room became quiet as Renae leaned forward in her seat to listen. *Wow,* she thought, *Shirley's sure got a big wardrobe. She's worn something different every time!*

Renae's glasses slid down her nose; she pushed them up. Then she remembered what Shirley had said in an earlier class about having one or two coordinating colors so that everything goes together. Sure enough, that jacket was from the pink-coral suit—and how well the geometric print of the dirndl and camisole matched it! She recognized the cute coral pumps, too. Almost against her will, Renae was being impressed by Shirley's "put-togetherness."

"As women," Shirley began, "we realize what makes the hard work of being a homemaker worthwhile. Of course, it's our relationships—the relationships we have with our spouse, our children, parents, friends, and the very unique

48   Managing to Be Free

relationship we all have been invited to enjoy with our heavenly Father.

"One of the reasons we worked on our personal priority sheets and listed last week's activities was to make sure we keep straight the threads of our lives. All must be woven to honor and please God, to form a person more and more like the Lord Jesus Christ.

"Edith Schaeffer, in her book *What Is a Family?*, compares a family to a mobile—moving, changing, constantly in motion, yet within the framework of a form. She says a family is 'unity and diversity, form and freedom, togetherness and individuality, and a Christian family is a mobile blown by the gentle breeze of the Holy Spirit.'

"It is important for us to recognize the *freedom*, the moving and changing; yet the *form* is what helps us hold it all together. And that's what we're working on here.

"You'll notice that one of the sheets being passed out now lists 'Susie Q's' objectives and priorities, and the other represents her weekly schedule. I hope you have brought pencils, your personal priority page, and your list of activities for last week, because we will be working directly with them today."

There was a general shuffling for purses. Renae glanced down at the papers just handed her and noticed that one represented "Susie Q's" detailed activities over a weekly period.

"Let me have your attention for just a moment," Shirley said. "First, be assured you do not have to make out a new schedule every week! Use just *one*, until circumstances or your responsibilities change. I usually make a new one every six months—sooner if something in my life changes drastically.

"Notice the sheet just handed you, titled 'Susie Q's Schedule.' Susie is a thirty-three-year-old housewife with three school-age children. Remember, even if your situation were exactly the same as hers, your schedule would be different because your priorities are different. Let's look at Susie's

Susie Q's Weekly Schedule

TIME	SUNDAY	MONDAY	TUESDAY	WED	THURSDAY	FRIDAY	SATURDAY
5:00							
6:00							
7:00	Devotions/ Breakfast	Personal Devotions 6:30-7:00 Cook Breakfast, Eat, Family Devotions					
8:00	Dinner Prep. Dress	Dinner prep., dishes Exercise, Shower, Dress					Personal Devotions
9:00		Straighten House					Breakfast Dishes Straighten House & Sunday Dinner prep.
10:00	Church	Laundry	Tuesday Class	Major Cleaning Project	House Cleaning	Beauty Shop & Grocery Store	
11:00							
12:00		Lunch Prep. for Tuesday class	Lunch	Lunch Phone Calls	Lunch	Errands	
1:00	Dinner & Guests	Laundry	Appointments or Rest	Catch-up		Lunch	Recreation with Family or Domestic Catch-up
2:00			Straighten House	Study for Wednesday Evening Class	Menu Planning	Preparation for Dinner Guests or Shopping with Children	
3:00	Rest Study for Couples Group	Children home from school, snack, discuss or catch-up. Homework/Chores					
4:00			4:30-6:30 Cook, Eat Clean-up	Dress Church Supper	4:30-6:30 Cook, Eat, Clean-up		
5:00	Dress Eat					Shower/ Dress Dinner Guests or out with Husband	Cook Eat Clean-up
6:00	Church & Couples	TV News		Wednesday Leadership Class	TV News		
7:00		Family			Correspondence and Personal Grooming		Family Night
8:00	Discipleship Group		Church Visitation				
9:00		Exercise, bath and bed by 10:00					Bed 10.00
10:00							
Add'l things to do			Take Deb to Ballet - 6:30 Elder's Dinner 3rd Tuesday at 5:30		Husband bowls. **Facial, nails, wardrobe upkeep	*Eat out with another couple once a month	

schedule. She can probably help us a great deal in understanding how to put our own together.

"Starting with Sunday morning, Susie gets up at 7:30, has her devotions; then she breakfasts and dresses. By 9:30 she's dressed and ready to go to church; she will come home at 12:30. You will note that she has already put the dinner in the oven, so when she gets home all she has to do is last-minute preparations. They have dinner. She rests from 2:00 to 3:00. At 3:00 she studies for her Sunday-evening class, at 4:30 she begins to dress. Then she has time marked out for dressing, eating, and church. At 10:00 P.M. she has scheduled exercise, bath, and bed.

"On Monday our Susie gets up at 6:30; has her personal devotions and breakfast. Then they have family devotions before the children go to school. By 8:30 she is ready to do the dishes and get dressed. Then she starts on the laundry and straightens the house. She usually begins dinner preparations in the morning, too. She stops for lunch because she has found she has a lot more energy in the afternoon if she stops, sits down, and has a bite, even if it's only leftovers. At 12:30 she prepares for her Tuesday class: maybe she's taking some needlepoint and wants to work on that, or it might be a Bible study."

The curly-haired redhead in front of Renae and Betty leaned over to her neighbor and in a loud whisper said, "How about a short nap or reading or relaxing?"

Renae grinned in sympathy, as Shirley continued: "Then Susie goes back to her laundry. From 3:00 to 3:30, she's given herself half an hour for unexpected activities: maybe just to catch up, to make some phone calls, and so on. When the children come home from school at 3:30, she's ready to discuss their day, help with homework, listen to their piano practice, whatever.

"At 4:30 she begins to cook. Since she had already started dinner in the morning, it only takes her about forty-five minutes to finish the preparations. Her husband comes home at 5:00; they eat dinner at 5:30. You'll see that she has allowed a total of two hours for cooking, eating, and cleaning up.

"At 6:30 Susie watches the evening TV news with her husband. One of her objectives, you will note, was to keep informed! Then she uses part of Monday evening for planning what they will be doing on their Friday 'family night.' Next come exercise and bath, as before, then bed at the usual hour."

For the first time, Betty seemed overwhelmed. "I couldn't stand it! Every moment seems filled," she said to Renae.

But Renae's eyes sparkled. "I can understand it now! It's like a puzzle," Renae blurted aloud and then turned dark red with embarrassment as heads swiveled in her direction.

Shirley smiled delightedly. "That's what I'm hoping for each of you! I'm glad it's beginning to come together for you, Renae."

They all looked down at Susie's schedule again as Shirley went on. "Tuesday starts off the same as Monday, except that she has her class at 9:00. She comes home for lunch, or sometimes goes out 'Dutch' with a friend or two, and takes a quick nap from 1:00 to 2:00."

"Yeah!" the young woman in the next row rejoiced under her breath.

"Or, if Susie is already out, she runs a few errands. She straightens the house from 2:00 to 3:00 if unable to do it in the morning. The rest is the same. Tuesday night they get a baby-sitter, and Susie and her husband do church visitation.

"Wednesday morning is the same until 9:00, when she has planned a special cleaning project. Noontime is lunch. Then she continues with the major project or spends the time in resting, phoning, visiting, or catching up. Susie's also in a Wednesday-evening fellowship class, so at 2:00 she gets busy on the homework for that. This is church-supper night, so instead of preparing dinner she and the children dress for the church supper and her fellowship class. There is a special program planned for the children at the same time. When she comes home, she reads for pleasure, for keeping her mental attitude positive.

"You can see that Thursday is housecleaning day for Susie, and as soon as her family leaves, she starts in. Lunch break, then finish cleaning."

"No rest," mourned the redhead. This time Shirley overheard her comment.

"Well, no," she answered. "No rest, but a refreshing change in activity. You see, at 2:00, Susie stops for menu planning, allowing herself an hour with the newspaper, scissors, and coupons. Her children come home at 3:30, and the rest of the afternoon goes as planned—except that Thursday night her husband goes bowling, and Susie allows time for family correspondence, including her mother and mother-in-law.

"Friday at 9:00 she heads for the beauty shop, then does her grocery shopping from the list she made Thursday afternoon. Friday night they have guests in for dinner. Right after lunch, she begins preparations for her dinner guests. And so the evening goes, with discussion and fellowship."

"I can't stand this heavy scheduling!" Betty said softly, with a frustrated sigh.

"Saturday the family sleeps late," Shirley observed. "In listing her objectives, Susie had decided she needed some sport, because her family is very sports-minded. The others are all very good at tennis, but she's a dud. So, after her devotions and breakfast, she's off to a tennis lesson at the Parks and Recreations Center."

"She sure does try hard!" Renae said.

"Then it's Little League, some family sport event, lunch, gardening, or general catch-up. Everybody works in the yard, or each one does his or her own thing. This is a good time for Susie to work on her recipe file or some other paper work. Saturday evening is a family night: they might cook out on the patio, pop corn, play games, or do some other shared activity.

"So-o-o-o-o-o, that's Susie's week! And with a few changes, it could probably be yours, too. We'll get started on your very own personalized schedule right away."

"Not mine, you won't!" Betty ground out softly to Renae. "I like space! I can stand less than a meticulous recipe file, but I cannot stand working every minute of the day and night!"

"You sure aren't in a good mood," Renae answered. "You seem to have switched places with me: that's what *I* said at first."

"To make out your weekly schedule," Shirley continued, "*Use pencil*—that's why I've given you two sheets, in case you change your mind about something."

Betty was obviously still upset at what she considered overly strict regimentation.

"Please get out the sheet of your last week's activities," Shirley suggested.

The women bent to pick up their purses and get out the needed materials. Shirley went on, "As soon as you get out your last week's activities sheet, take a look at it with three questions in mind, as listed on one of the sheets I've passed out.

Pertinent Priority Questions

1. Did I get done everything I wanted to do?
2. Did I do things together that belong together—like errands and shopping and the library?
3. How can I improve my use of time?

"This is where your list of priorities is going to help you, since we each know now what is most important to us and that it needs to fit into the time available. The question is mostly 'How do I fit all this I have to do into this twenty-four hour segment of time—and not leave anything out?' And probably some of you are adding under your breath, 'And not be completely worn out!'"

The redhead interrupted Shirley to say, "The only reason I'd want a schedule is to get, uh, mundane things out of the way as quickly and easily as possible so I can have time for myself and for people. I *want* to leave out anything I can get away with leaving out—that's what I call 'simplicity' and that's what I want!"

Renae and Betty looked at each other, and Betty smiled defensively. "I agree with that girl!" They had already compared both their priority and schedule pages, commenting on how different each one's week had turned out. Renae wondered again how all this "homework" was going to help her, but she was willing to give it a try.

"What did we see last week as our first priority, ladies?" Shirley asked.

A chorus of voices answered, "God."

"Right," Shirley said. "So, on your fresh sheet, mark in *first* the time you're going to spend alone with God in prayer and Bible study. Remember that we agreed it might be different for those who have small babies, who live alone, who have job responsibilities, and so on. Don't copy what your neighbor writes down; her lifestyle is different from yours.

"The reason we first mark in our time with God is because we are building our whole schedule around him. He is first in our lives.

"Next mark in your getting-up time. This is determined by your time alone with God if you've picked the time before anyone else is up. Otherwise, what you have to get done before the first family member leaves in the morning would be the determining factor.

"For example, my son is the first one out of the house, at seven. Before he leaves, it is our family custom to have breakfast and family devotions together. So I get up at six."

There were some soft groans and funny comments, and Renae felt resentful. "I don't like *anyone* telling me what to do, or when, or how," she muttered to Betty.

But Betty only looked at her and said, "That's your decision, but I'm glad for any help I can get. I sure think you'd be, too. That's what you said earlier!"

"Well," Renae jabbed her pencil point through the paper, "I'm not now!"

"Next," Shirley went on, "you'll want to mark in your bedtime." Hoots of laughter answered her statement, but she only smiled unperturbed.

"Really, I mean it! I need eight hours of sleep. To get up at six and get eight hours of sleep, one must go to bed at ten the night before. Sleep requirements vary with each individual. Decide how much sleep you need and set your bedtime accordingly.

"Those of you who are here obviously don't have jobs outside the home, and I'm very glad for you. However, if any of you is sharing these home-priority management ideas with a working friend, this would be the time for her to mark in her job hours. And I'd like to pause here to say that although it usually doesn't really pay for a woman to work when she has a husband *and* children at home, many women don't have that choice. They just have to work. There could be many reasons: illness of her partner, divorce, death, just not enough pay from one check to maintain the family, and so on.

"Jill Briscoe, the author-speaker, once was told by a missionary friend, 'You and your husband must find out how you can minister most effectively, both as a couple and individually. Stop trying to copy us. Whatever it takes, learn your own way of serving the Lord and keeping your marriage strong.' Of course, for any of us, for any Christian, the bottom-line question involved in any decision is: 'Does *God* want me to do this?'

"As we remember the biblical principles we discussed earlier, we know God created Eve as a helpmeet to Adam. And a helpmeet helps her husband meet the situations in his life. She helps meet his needs. Physical. Social. Mental and emotional. Spiritual. And financial.

"Our responsibility as married women is to encourage our husbands and support them emotionally. It's the oneness—the being a part of his life—that's important. So, whatever role God wants you to have, that's what you need to do. Remember, God can, and does, custom-design jobs to fit your special needs.

"One thing we need to do is support and encourage God's working women, to free them from the guilt some people are loading on them, to help them in the areas we can. For example, maybe you can offer to be responsible for the children after school a day a week and give them supper, so a working friend can have a bit of time off. If you ask the Lord, I know he'll give you creative ideas about this.

"And, from my long-ago experience, I'd just like to tell every working woman that it's okay to take short cuts. To let things go somewhat. To hire help for the house. To ask her husband—if she has one—for special assistance. If she brings in part of the income, he must do part of the work of maintaining the house and nurturing. I'd also emphasize that she should train her children to do for themselves things that are within their capability.

"These women who have to work are very special and need our support and encouragement in every possible way. And remind yourself to be thankful that you can stay home and be a mother and housewife! Both you and I and our working sisters are seeking to be all God wants us to be.

"Now, back with our schedules. Fill in your family time. Checking again with your priority lists, you'll remember who is first there. Yes, your husband. So plan time alone with him—maybe a weekly night out. Then plan to do something special *for* him each week—a back rub, his favorite meal, sharing a cartoon or poem with him. Let it be something that only *you* know he likes. I'm sure you've found, as I have, that good intentions are not enough. If I'm going to do something, I need to decide what and when.

"Schedule time alone with each child at least once a week—you could take your daughter along grocery shopping or take your son alone to Little League, talking in the car with him. Take a walk with your children or just sit on their beds and talk. Any activity you do *alone* with each child, with all your attention on him or her, will let them know that they are special. Of course, also plan time for family devotions, family fun night, shared family activities.

"And while you're thinking about your family, how about your parents or parents-in-law? Schedule time to phone them, to write a note, or to have a meal with them if they live near enough."

A short, plump woman in a bright cherry-colored jumpsuit stood up. Her bushy white hair bobbed as she said excitedly, "Wait a minute, Shirley. You're going too fast for me!" Others in the crowd nodded sympathetically when she continued, "I'm about to give up on this schedule."

Shirley smiled, knowing how many times she herself had felt like that. Gently she went on: "Don't worry about it. I'm just hurrying through what has to be done right now. When I finish, we'll pass out a sheet of instructions to help you complete your schedule. But I want to go through it all with you first."

Renae took a deep breath; she was overwhelmed, too.

"Remember, too, that energy levels are different. There are high-energy people and low-energy people. And sometimes the high-energy people demand too much from those with less stamina. There are also specific times in our lives when we may be one or the other. So be patient with each other; and, as Paul tells us in Ephesians 4:32, '. . . be kind to one another, tenderhearted, forgiving each other, just as God in Christ also has forgiven you.'"

There was a general sigh of relief as Shirley went on: "Are there days when you feel like your house is a mess [she threw up her hands as if in desperation] from one end to the other?"

As laughter swept through the room, she said, "*Now,* you're ready to include homemaking on your schedule. Think of all the specific duties involved. To help you, I've included a list on the next sheet that is titled 'Specific Homemaking Duties.'

Specific Homemaking Activities

Daily

1. Beds
2. Clutter picked up
3. Dishes washed and kitchen clean
4. Bathrooms
5. Meal preparation

Weekly or Every Other Week

1. Vacuum
2. Mop
3. Dust and polish furniture
4. Shopping and errands
5. Change bed linen
6. Clean stove and refrigerator (day before shopping)
7. Laundry
8. Menu planning
9. Baking
10. Sewing (or hobby)

Periodically

1. Wash curtains
2. Clean windows/woodwork
3. Clean out closets/drawers
4. Shampoo carpets
5. Polish silver
6. Put away out-of-season clothes

"Think of things like laundry, general housecleaning, special cleaning projects, grocery shopping, menu planning, baking, sewing, and so on. They all need to be put into your schedule if you're going to get them done!"

"Will you remember as you consider the activities that these are *guidelines*? Add any other activities to your schedule that are specific to your own situation." Shirley paused, then continued, "There are two other priorities we have mentioned, and it seems to me that they might be somewhat flexible and interchangeable. Can anyone think which ones I mean?"

A girl in the front row asked, "Do you mean 'myself' and 'ministry'?"

"Exactly," Shirley answered. "It may seem hard, at first, to make out a schedule for either of these priorities and stick to it, but eventually it should become second nature—freeing you for more exciting and creative pursuits.

"First we try to answer that question, 'What about me?' We all need some just-for-myself time—a chance to refresh our bodies and tend to personal grooming. Aside from its intrinisic benefits, how we feel affects how we look to others. Our appearance, as well as our actions, reflects our attitudes and can be a positive influence in our ministry to others.

"Anne Ortlund, in her book *The Disciplines of the Beautiful Woman*, has made an interesting evaluation of Proverbs 31, which describes God's ideal woman. She says—and you can check it when you get home—only one verse out of the twenty-two describes how she looked, but—she looked great!

"If we use about five percent of our time on our looks, we can give a little over an hour a day to this priority. The next sheet shows how my daily hour for myself is spent. Yours might be slightly different, but I think you get the point."

As the women looked at Shirley's schedule, she commented, "This simple routine takes little time and keeps me from going to seed.

"Of course, you will want to include 'dressing' on your schedule. The secret to being able to limit the time needed for that is to have few clothes to choose from! I keep my closet stripped down to things I enjoy wearing—and that fit *now.* And if something's there, it is clean and ready to wear. Out-of-season and special-occasion clothing is in another closet. Things needing repair go to the sewing room."

My Daily Hour for Myself

Morning: exercise, shower, blow-dry my hair, make up my face. This takes forty-five minutes.

Bedtime: exercise, soak in the tub, cream my legs and elbows, etc. Makes me relax and feel wonderful. Takes twenty minutes.

Once a Week: I do my nails, give myself a facial (while I'm in the tub), and check over my wardrobe.

Once a Month: I get a haircut.

Renae almost groaned audibly. *I could never achieve that kind of organization!* she thought. *Besides, there are umpteen outfits in my two closets and some in Steve's, too.*

But Shirley was continuing, and Renae had already decided she would listen carefully to what Shirley had to say. "I didn't really mean to discuss this right now, but now that I've started, let me just add a few more grooming ideas before we go on with our schedules.

"First, though, I must remind you that there is nothing in your background or genes that dooms you to live out your days in a mess! You *are* capable of putting your own life in order and of meeting the constant challenge of managing your home priorities.

"There is a principle in all this. *To manage your time, eliminate clutter and concentrate on your priorities.* This means that to keep a sharp wardrobe, eliminate the unnecessary and concentrate on a few right-for-you outfits in one or two color schemes. To discover your best colors, see *Color Me Beautiful*, the paperback book by Carole Jackson published by Ballantine. There are, of course, grooming ideas in other books and magazines, too. Check into them if you need help.

"Remember, 'our flesh clothes His presence!' Isn't that exciting! If we have the Lord's presence in our hearts, he will glow through our faces. Not our clothes, but our hearts, will be the focus of attention!"

There was a short pause before Shirley continued. "Now I'd like to think with you about ministry. In her thoughtful little book, *Eighth Day of Creation*, Elizabeth O'Conner says,

> We ask to know the will of God without guessing that His will is written into our very beings. We perceive that will when we discern our gifts. Our obedience and surrender to God is in large part our obedience and surrender to our gifts.

"My ministry is my life and walk with God. Ministry changes hourly. At one time, God might nudge me to walk across the street and chat with the widow who is my neighbor. At another time, ministry might simply mean helping one of my children with homework. The only way we'll know what God wants is to listen for and hear his voice, moment by moment.

"For our purposes in making out the schedule, I am using the word *ministry* to mean all that, as well as my calling or vocation, such as painting, sewing for others, or arranging field trips, and church work.

"Ministry comes *after* the family and home in priority, because I learned early that I could not effectively minister to others if I was neglecting my responsibilities as wife, mother, and homemaker. If relationships were strained at home and there were tensions caused by my lack of planning or being physically drained from being out of the home too much, God was not honored by the good works I was trying to do for others.

"There was a time when I felt my children lived in the nursery and I lived at the church. This was when God began teaching me the primary importance of my calling as a wife and mother. He also used my desire to minister to others to motivate me to find more effective ways of managing my time. He wanted to bring balance into my life.

"Now, on your weekly schedule, please mark in time for *your* ministry and meetings. Include such things as church attendance, visitation, study time, if you teach, and fellowship group meetings. If most of your ministry time is spent in going to meetings, rather than in touching lives, ask God to give you some individuals to share your life with.

"Then mark in all the other meetings to which you're committed—you know, PTA, Gray Lady, garden club, school clinic, and so on. If you're away from home too much, start eliminating here.

"Some women, of course, do not like belonging to things. Perhaps you are happier in solitary pursuits. God has given each of us special personalities and aptitudes. To be true to the way he has made us is to be true to him."

Everyone joined in Shirley's sigh when she had finished her explanation of the sheets they had been given. "The schedule is pretty full, isn't it?" she commented with a smile. "I think every woman has a crowded schedule! One answer might be to drop some of the low-priority things you can let go of as unnecessary baggage. But you're already on the road to success because you have taken the first two important steps. You have figured out your purposes and your priorities, and you have tentatively planned your days."

"Well," Betty sighed explosively, "I feel considerably better now!"

"Incidentally," Shirley added, a twinkle in her eyes, "you'll see that the last page in this set of worksheets is a summary of what we just went over, 'How to Make a Weekly Schedule.'"

There was a rustle of papers as the women shuffled through their handouts.

"We're through right on time today," Shirley finished, smiling. "Next week, we'll get into the nitty-gritty of eliminating clutter, what I call 'working around a room' and organizing what's left.

How to Make a Weekly Schedule

1. Mark in the time you're going to spend alone with God.
2. Mark in getting-up time.
3. Mark in bedtime.
4. Fill in your family time:
   a. husband
   b. time alone with each child
   c. family devotions, activities, fun night
   d. parents
   Note: If you are a working woman, job schedule comes next.
5. Schedule your homemaking. (See "Specific Homemaking Duties.")
6. Plan time for yourself. This should not be left out. It can usually be flexible, **but be sure to put It In!** Include exercise, rest, hair and wardrobe care, a hobby or sport.
7. Ministry and church activities are filled in last:
   a. church attendance
   b. visitation
   c. study time, if you teach
   d. fellowship group meetings
   Add all other meetings to which you are committed (such as PTA, Gray Ladies, garden club, school clinic, etc).

"And now, before you leave, I'd like to remind you to be sure to take home the new handouts to read this week. They will help you in completing your schedule. 'Bye for now."

7

Renae Walks on the Beach

It was dusk. Renae was restless. The room was filled with reflections of the dying sun. The house was silent, and she shivered as if she were dying of cold, listening to the emptiness around her. Her daughters were off at a friend's house for another overnight party.

"Really," she said silently, exasperated with herself, "I ought to start saying 'no' to some of these things. Kathy and Melissa are out too much! Although, I have to admit, the time the group was here, they were all very good and easy to manage."

A small smile curved her lips and she shrugged. She guessed she was just being "unreasonable." Again! She could almost hear Kathy saying it.

A sudden flare of sunset color found her desk, still as messy as ever. She glared at its clutter, wondering why she could never seem to settle down to correspondence or chores. Now she felt lonely and like bursting into tears.

A thin edge of irritation bordered the restlessness like a dark piping. *Why, why, did Steve have to choose this specific time to be gone—and with that new female client?* Renae remembered that first meeting. She had dropped into Steve's office, hoping to lunch with him—but he was just leaving with the new client. They had invited her, so she had tagged along.

"Jeanette," the woman said her name was, although Renae bet herself a doughnut that it was probably just plain "Jean."

But there was nothing plain about Jeanette! From the top of the long blond hair coiled crownlike on her head, to the tiny red-painted toenails that showed through her fashionable sandals, Jeanette was lovely. She was refined and talented, too. Her blue eyes sparkled when she talked about her new job—which was what she was *supposed* to be consulting Steve about.

Renae's heels beat a sharp tattoo on the wood floor as she walked to the window, glanced out, and walked back across the rug to her desk. Suddenly her mind was made up. There was no reason for her to stay here and mope. She would go to the beach!

After parking the car by a row of bathhouses, she walked over a dune to a narrow strip of sand. The sun had sunk now and the horizon was less fiercely colored. The clouds were swept into gray masses with rough streaks of flame running between them—like chiffon scarves, she thought fancifully.

She took off her sandals and let the sand, still warm from the afternoon sun, squish through her toes. An occasional high-reaching wave curled around her ankles. There was the lingering smell of seaweed and dead fish, but all swept clean by the wind from the sea.

Renae walked nearly a mile. The roar of the surf quieted to a slow, sad whisper farther and farther away as the sea began to withdraw once more. Points of light glittered across its troubled surface from the light of a rising, lopsided moon.

She flopped down on her back and looked at the sky. There was a faint ring around the moon. A "harbinger of disaster," she remembered reading somewhere. Her thoughts hopscotched around her mind, trying not to land on what was really bothering her. Finally she admitted to herself that the girls were not the problem. Not really. Not even Steve's being with Jeanette. *Though I don't particularly like it,* she thought.

Shirley's class! That's what it was! Oh, not that business about priorities and housekeeping. She knew she needed all that. "The Lord—" The word skittered off the edge of her mind and she changed it to "goodness knows."

Renae stopped thinking and watched a sailboat tacking back and forth across the moon path. She scarcely realized she'd been holding her breath until it all came out in a rush when the boat grounded on the beach, its sails flapping, its sailors tiny silhouettes edged in silver.

Like the sails, Renae's thoughts fluttered back and forth in her mind.

She realized that there was something different about the women who met in Shirley's class. "I'm not sure I want to be different, anyway," she argued with herself. "But I've always wondered if I were missing out on something, even though I did accept Christ as a child. If what Shirley says is true, I've been missing out on a whole lot!

"I know all the usual Sunday-school stories. But I wish I knew the Bible better. Really, what I wish is, is—I wish I knew God the way Shirley does—and some of the other women there, too. I wish I could ask him something—and hear him answer me!"

Suddenly she stood up, walked swiftly to the receding sea's edge, then retraced her steps more slowly back up the beach to the dunes. *Hear him answer me,* her thoughts echoed.

The words slapped at the dark fears and secret longings of her mind like the tiny waves slapping the rocks farther out. She watched as they sent up bright phosphorescent droplets that seemed to hang against the night sky like miniature fireworks. *Hear him answer me. Hear him answer me.*

Renae dropped to her knees and started to pray aloud shyly, her voice sounding strange in her own ears.

"Dear God, I hardly know what to say to you. Shirley says you made us and you love us and you have a plan for us. And I know it's true. But—I'm sorry I haven't tried to talk to you before. Will you answer me, please, and show me how I can be the woman you want me to be? I didn't even know that you wanted me to be Steve's helpmeet or any of that. I want to learn, though. Please tell me what to do. Thank you."

She finished off quickly with "in Jesus' Name, Amen," like they did in Shirley's class every week. Somehow, tears were sliding down her cheeks. She brushed at them with a sandy hand, then giggled to think what she must look like. She wasn't sure how she expected God to answer. She just knew that he would. And she felt all quiet inside—and warm—and loved.

The waves lapped gently at the shore and the wind ruffled her hair as she walked back toward the car.

8

Eliminating Household Clutter

Is this the right place, Betty?" Renae blurted at the door to the conference room. "What a mess!" she went on as they sat down. "It looks like a cyclone hit it—just like my living room after the girls get home from school!"

With a swirl of her pastel-striped dirndl, Shirley moved into the center of the confusion. "I'm sure none of your homes looks like this! I exaggerated the problem so it would be easier for us all to see how it can be solved."

Renae almost bit her tongue, her teeth clamping shut on her own last words. Betty shot her an amused glance; "See, nobody's living room is this bad!" Renae wrinkled up her nose, then listened as Shirley began the day's lesson.

"The secret is that you have to concentrate on individual tasks," she said. "You can't sit down first thing to read a book or talk on the telephone. There's time for that, but in the middle of chaos, they're a waste of time! And when you

finish wasting time, that housework will still be waiting for
you! Doesn't your mind get tired just *thinking* of all you have
to do? Before you know it, you're tailspinning into a mild
form of depression.

"So, get right up and *attack!* Just look at that windowsill
with the miscellaneous bottles of half-used—what? Po-
tions? And that stack of newspapers on the floor. Piles of
magazines on top of every available flat surface. Too much
furniture in the room. Toys scattered all around. And the rest
of this stuff—Hmmm, I wonder when that wooly sweater
was last worn? Doesn't it look 'interesting'?"

Renae and Betty watched Shirley heft a laundry basket, a
big brown paper sack, and some large cardboard boxes.
Betty's surprised comment burst into the stillness, "Those
look like *pear* boxes!"

"They are," Shirley answered Betty's exclamation. "I like
pear boxes because they have lids. Apple boxes, too." She
pushed the containers into the center of the make-believe
living room.

"These," she paused and pointed dramatically, "are my
eliminators! I call them that because they help me eliminate
clutter. Remember, please, that although I have only one so-
called room to show you today, in your own home you will
want to go systematically from room to room with the clutter eliminators.

"Soiled clothing and linen go in the laundry basket. Trash
goes into the paper bag. And—you can see that I have labeled
the boxes 'giveaway,' 'store,' 'kids,' 'linen closet,' and so on—
the boxes are for those items. As you work in your home,
you will possibly have a box for almost every room.

"Tricia, will you please take the laundry basket? Nancy,
put the trash in the paper bag. And, and, why don't *you*"—To
her dismay, Renae realized that Shirley was looking straight
at her.

"I'm sorry I don't know your name." Shirley paused long
enough for Renae to answer, then went on. "When the others

have finished, will you come up and we'll work together on filling the pear boxes.

"All right, Tricia and Nancy. May I suggest that the quickest way to unclutter a room, is around-the-clock. You know, working a circle around the room. Because there are two of you helping me, I'm going to ask you to work both clockwise and counterclockwise this time.

"Tricia, why don't you go around the perimeter of the room to the right, and Nancy, you go to the left, each doing your thing. You'll meet in the center. And when the rest of you are at home, circle your room in whichever direction is best for you. While you work, I'll just go on with a few suggestions.

"Never concentrate entirely on one room at a time. That's dangerous. You'll simply get bogged down in one room.

"Now, *quick!*—You *are* moving quickly, aren't you?—load the washer with clothes, empty the trash, and—Renae, would you come up and help me, please? We're ready for our eliminator boxes. And that's exactly what we are going to do: eliminate unused clothing, toys, excess what-nots, and furniture.

"When I was a schoolteacher, I kept noticing how neat and orderly my friend Evelyn's schoolroom was. One day I went home with her, and her house was the same way. So I asked her, 'Evelyn, you're as busy as I am; how do you keep things so in order?'

"She answered, 'It's simple: I discovered that the less I have, the less I have to keep neat. Everything has to be either useful or beautiful, or I get rid of it. And when I started teaching school, I followed that same principle.'

"Well, I tell you, I went home and started stripping my house. I, too, eliminated everything that did not serve a function or add beauty to a room. Just a word here on 'beauty.' Although we can work on improving our taste, one's perception of what is beautiful is always personal. If you like it, keep it.

"Now, as to function—in my house the bedroom is for sleeping and resting. So I removed all the items that destroyed the restful function of the room. I've found this same system works throughout the house: in the rooms themselves, in the closets, on the shelves. I ask myself questions like 'Have I used this in the last year?' or 'Does it have some special value to me, sentimental or monetary?' And—Beware of this one! It can catch you even when you have really decided to get rid of things—'Could it come in handy someday?'

"Even if my answer to *that* question is 'yes,' I usually put the article in the throw-away or give-away box. That word *someday* almost always means I am hanging on to clutter.

"Here we go, Renae. What about this sweater?"

Renae began doubtfully, "Well, it's too small for either of my girls—and it looks too bad to wear, really."

"Right! Into the trash it goes. These children's books and toys?"

"Into the box marked 'kids'? And this pile of business papers had better go into the den on hubby's desk." Renae was beginning to enjoy herself. "And look at these paper napkins. Shouldn't they go into the kitchen? And these dirty glasses and cups, too."

"That's the idea," Shirley agreed. "You can see how easy it is when you get started. Thanks, Renae. That's all for now. And just like I told Tricia and Nancy, you would move around the room. Pick a starting point and then work more or less in a circle. You can see that's a good way to avoid backtracking and moving to and fro."

As she returned to her place, Renae thought, *It really is easier than it seems. I hope she gives us printed directions; I know I won't remember all these ideas!*

At the same time Shirley commented, "You're all such good listeners that I don't want to bore you, so—we'll pass out today's work papers now."

Renae giggled. Catching a surprised look from Betty, she defended, "I was just thinking that!"

"Perhaps the best way will be to read through them together," Shirley said. "I'll be making comments from time to time, and if any of you have a question, please just raise your hand or call my name.

"Now, the first sheet is titled, 'The Clutter Eliminators,' and it is what we just went over."

The Clutter Eliminators

The Three Boxes
1. The throw-away box
2. The give-away box
3. The someplace else box

The Three Questions
1. Have I used this in the last year?
2. Does it have some special value to me, sentimental or functional?
3. Could it come in handy someday?

Note: Periodically, I go through every room, closet, and drawer in my house with the three boxes and the three questions to help me decide.

Renae and the rest of the women looked at the top paper that had just been handed to them.

Renae sighed. "It looks so simple, written down like this," she told Betty. "And it was even easy to do when I was helping Shirley unclutter the room up there. But I'm not sure I can do it by myself at home."

"The next thing, of course," Shirley went on, "is to take the boxes to their eventual location. Don't try to organize all your closets or shelves at once. Just shove the boxes inside the closet doors, if possible. Slip books into any available bookshelf, put papers into the office area, put clothes into the appropriate closet, and toys and games in the children's rooms.

"I want you to listen now, very closely. This is probably the most important thing I've said today. Please let me see all your eyes. Good!" Shirley paused, then continued emphatically: "*Don't try to do it all at once. It took you a while to get where you are. It will take you a while to get where you want to be.*

"Work at a pace of ten minutes, half an hour, or one or two hours at a time. Decide beforehand which it will be, and when the time you have designated is up, quit! If it's a closet you're working on, concentrate on the lower left-hand shelves one day, the upper ones another day. The same goes if you are working on the refrigerator.

"Remember how we always say to the children not to take such big bites? 'Just bite off as much as you can chew,' we insist. Well, do the same as you go about eliminating clutter in your house! Bite off as much of a job as you can do in the time you've allotted yourself."

Relief showed in the faces of some of the women, who obviously had been wondering how they could handle the big job of face-lifting their homes all at once.

"My plan today is to go over ideas I've found helpful in eliminating clutter, in organizing what is left in closets and drawers, and in developing orderliness. Remember that this is the way *I* do things; the way that has worked out best for *me*. Take the ideas that are helpful to you and discard the rest, or at least let them simmer until you are ready for them."

Shirley put down the work pages and held up a hardcover book. "In this book, *Psychocybernetics,* Dr. Maxwell Maltz proved scientifically that an idea must be repeated for twenty-one consecutive days before it becomes permanently fixed in the subconscious. That's how habits are made. So, if you really mean business about changing your home priorities, you'll have to start by making up your mind to establish new habits.

"Maybe you'll want to stick up a list of your goals on the refrigerator, so that every time you walk by you'll see and be reminded of it. Why not post the page of 'The Clutter Eliminators' on your refrigerator when you go home today? Then, for the next three weeks, try following this system—and see what happens!"

"That's a good idea," Renae said to Betty. "I think I'll try it."

"Sure, pretty soon it will hurt our brains to step over something instead of picking it up!" Betty answered with a teasing smile.

9

Organizing What's Left

Shirley pushed some of the furniture of her temporary "room" over to one side to give herself more space. Then she turned around one of the supposed walls to show a large drawing prepared earlier. It was of a beautifully arranged closet.

Organizing Closets and Drawers

First, decide what to hang in closets and what to fold in drawers, and shift clothes accordingly.

1. To organize drawers:
   a. Put the most frequently used items (such as underwear) in the most accessible spot.
   b. Subdivide some categories, such as sweaters, filmy lingerie, and ordinary underwear, into their natural divisions of "frequently worn" and "less frequently worn."
2. To divide drawers:
   a. Use small boxes such as candy and shoe.
      EXAMPLE: separate a child's socks from underwear by using a box to hold one category.
   b. Egg cartons or plastic ice cube trays make good jewelry and earring holders.
3. To create additional drawer space:
   a. Use bookcase shelves, curtained or screened.
   b. Consider stackable plastic or vinyl storage cubes.

"The next area we want to look at," Shirley said with a bright smile, "flows out of what we just did. It's covered on your second set of today's sheets and is titled, 'Arranging Closets and Drawers.' As you can see from the sketch, a beautifully arranged closet is a joy.

"Remember what we've done so far. First, we eliminated the clutter, using our boxes and helping questions. That done, it's time now to put the closets—and drawers, too—in order. Look at the top sheet of the set."

In an aside to Betty, Renae said, "You don't use bookcases for drawer space if you're bookaholics like us! But it *is* a good idea for some!"

"Maybe I should explain about 'My Treasure Box.' The Treasure Box is simply an empty cardboard box covered with stick-on paper or cloth. For the husband and wife, a Treasure Box might include love letters, special keepsakes and awards, and such. Treasure Boxes are kept in the closet of each person's bedroom. For a child, it is a keepsake box for a

---

Women's Closets

1. Hang your clothes according to category:
   a. blouses together
   b. skirts together
   c. slacks together
   d. pant suits together
   e. casual dresses together
   f. dressy dresses together
   g. long dresses together

   Note: • Consider multiple hangers for blouses, skirts, pants, etc.
   • Use a clothes rack such as stores use, hidden with a decorative screen.
   • Use a parallel second clothing rod to double closet space for short items such as blouses and skirts.
   • Garment bags are awkward, take up valuable space and block clothes from view: reserve them for fragile garments of lace or chiffon.

2. Keep a list posted in your closet showing which accessories you can wear with each outfit. This saves time when you're dressing.
3. To make vacuuming easier, I keep shoes off the floor on shoe racks or in shoe bags.
4. Shelves above clothing rods can be used to
   a. keep purses lined up so all can be seen.
   b. store labeled shoe boxes with seldom-used items such as winter boots or special occasion shoes.
   c. have an attractively decorated pasteboard box called "My Treasure Box," containing special personal keepsakes like love letters, school awards, personal baby book, Mother's Day cards, etc.
   d. store personal sports equipment and/or luggage.
   e. Try to have a full-length mirror in your closet or bedroom for checking your appearance.

---

baby book, special papers, selected schoolwork from each year of his or her life, especially awards and treasures. I have found that we all love to browse through our Treasure Boxes. And they become a source of remembrance and fond memories, especially for children, when they are grown.

"Next we'll take a look at 'Men's Closets,'" Shirley said. "And don't get discouraged, thinking you'll never to able to get it all done. Remember the Spanish proverb, *'Poco a poco se va lejos'*—you know, little by little you go a long way! And when you actually get down to working on your closets and drawers, why you'll only do a bit at a time. And before you know it, they'll be organized!"

Men's Closets

1. Hang clothes according to category.
   a. suits together
   b. pants together (on hangers covered with cardboard to eliminate creases)
   c. dress shirts together
   d. casual shirts together
   e. grubbies or play clothes together
2. Arrange shoes on racks or in shoe bags.
3. Shelves above clothes to hold
   a. hats and caps
   b. shoeshine kit
   c. Treasure Box
   d. personal luggage and sports equipment

The redhead sitting in front of Betty and Renae looked back at them with a cheeky grin and commented, "I'm sure glad I have only *one* man to work on!" They each had been thinking the same thing and smiled back at her as Shirley started to explain the 'Men's Closets' work page.

"For those of you who have children, this next section is especially important. I know that you'll see the same general rules apply as to all the other closets, but I have added some special ideas to help our children help themselves. Look now at the next page with me, please."

"That was pretty detailed, wasn't it?" Shirley asked. "I want to remind you again here that some of you may already have your own way of organizing. That's great. Or you may want to pick up one or two ideas from these sheets. That's great, too. From the ideas I'm giving you, use the ones that will help you the most. Make them a part of your lifestyle and let them work for you.

"Before we go on to the next pages, I'd like to emphasize that knowing when to stop is as important as knowing when and where to start! Everyone has what we used to call at school a 'different task-toleration level.' One person can concentrate productively on a single project for hours, while

Children's Closets

1. Organize children's closets in the same way as your own, but here are some special suggestions that might be helpful.
2. Lower racks for small children (so they can hang up their own clothes) by hanging a broom handle by chains from hooks under the shelf.

CLOTHES RACK

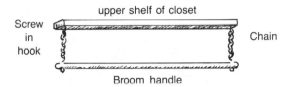

upper shelf of closet

Screw in hook

Chain

Broom handle

FOR CHILDREN

3. Shelves above clothes rack can house seldom-used items such as sleeping bags, large toys, Treasure Box, etc.
4. Make an attractive toy box by covering a large carton with cloth or wall paper. Keep it handy for toys.
5. Inside closet:
   a. build narrow shelves on side wall between back of closet and door jamb to hold books, small toys and dolls, games, shoes (if you do not use a shoe rack).
   b. Or place a small bookcase under hanging clothes to accomplish the same objective.
   c. Small, loose toy pieces can be placed in open shoe boxes for easy visibility or placed in a cloth drawstring bag and hung from a nail inside the closet.
6. Get everything up off the floor for easy cleaning!

another gets woozy and sloppy after one hour. And, of course, different projects make different types of demands. Let your personal response be the key. When your muscles and brain cells are aching—quit!

"The more effort I continue to put into a project after I've reached my sensible quitting point, the less value I get out of it. Overreaching also causes me to dread and procrastinate the next time something has to be done. This is something to remember about jobs you delegate to your children, too."

There was a question nagging Renae's mind, but she
didn't quite feel like asking it. Then a dark-haired young
woman spoke up, "What do you do with the things you need
to remove from the house because you don't have room for
them, but they're good things that you want to keep for
future use?"

"That's a good question," Shirley answered. "That's when
you discover the joy of a garage. Or an attic. I use some more
pear or apple boxes to put all those things that I need to keep
for the future—like Christmas decorations, artificial
flowers, my coffee urn, even outgrown children's clothes—if
I think I may have another child or to give to a friend's child
later. I use gummed labels to mark the contents of each box.
That way, if I want to remove the contents and reuse the box,
all I have to do is change the label. And—this is the big
plus—I can go to the garage and immediately find whatever I
want. Of course, if I can find something when I need it, that
saves me a lot of time, too."

One of the women a couple of rows in front of Renae and
Betty said, "If I could be convinced all this would work and
save me time, I'd do almost anything!" Several others nodded, and Shirley answered, "All I can tell you is that it
worked for me."

In the next-to-the front row, an arm shot up into the air
and a voice with a distinct southern accent said, "Shirley,
may I?—"

"Of course, Kim. Why don't you come up and share what
you've found to be of benefit to you?" As a tall girl in bright
nautical blue stood up, Shirley went on to explain: "Kim is
one of the women who has already gone through this seminar."

Renae watched Kim go forward confidently. "Crisp and
clean" were the words to describe Kim, Renae decided approvingly and shifted in her seat to listen better.

"When Shirley first explained about her system, I was one
of those who said, 'Boy, a schedule's not for me! I'm just not
geared that way!' You see, I used to work at an outside job and

I felt tied-up, bound-down, and completely frustrated by my schedule. I had to think so far ahead when I was working, even planning meals a week in advance, that I sure didn't want *another* schedule! Once I wasn't working, I wanted to be a lady of leisure. And if I didn't want to wash today, then I wouldn't wash. Tomorrow, or whenever, would be good enough!

"One night I told Freddie—he's my husband—'Guess what Shirley's got us doing now? One of our disciplines is our homework. See! She told us to write down a schedule and I'm going to, but I don't ever intend to use it.'"

Kim's feelings paralleled Renae's so exactly that she leaned forward, eager to hear how Kim's husband had responded.

"And this is what Freddie said," Kim's short brown hair bobbed as she giggled merrily, "He said, 'Hand it to me and I'll write it out for you and then maybe you can get everything done.'

"Well! That was sort of a slap in the face, and all I said was, 'thanks!'

"The next class I told Shirley I'd gotten it written out just because she had told us to. Shirley reminded me that because I had chosen to accept the discipline of coming to the class, she had become, in this, my line of authority." Kim's expressive face became serious as she added, "I told her about Freddie, too, that it looked to me like Freddie really cared. I figured then—since he wanted to help me, and Shirley was trying to help by teaching the class—the least I could do was try.

"And I found that the schedule really works for me. Just getting up fifteen minutes earlier in the morning completely changed my life. It gave me time with the Lord and gave me time to get my family up on time so they weren't all rushing around madly. I made out my menus and did my shopping. Monday there was time for me to wash. My house was so in order that I had time to do everything Shirley had helped me put on a schedule. When a friend called and asked me to have lunch with her, I had time to do that, too!

"And Freddie is *really* happy!"

The ladies applauded as Kim returned to her seat. Renae thought guiltily, *I'm sure Steve would like me to get on a schedule, too. I wonder if I can.*

Shirley smiled, saying, "Thank you, Kim. It's always helpful to hear about others in the same situation. Kim's husband was her deciding motivation. And your husband may be the motivation you need, too. Or, like me, maybe you want to get it organized because you know you have too much to do and you can't do it the way you're heading now."

10

A Place for Everything—
And Everything in Its Place!

L ook at the next set of sheets, stapled together at the top," Shirley continued, picking up some papers from the table. "You'll see that each sheet is headed 'A Place for Everything.'

"This is a basic principle for order, if you add the important second clause, 'And Everything in Its Place!' It is relatively easy to keep a thing in its place and to get your family to cooperate with you if they know where things belong.

"What are some of the places we should establish in the home for storing items? I have found several storage places to be valuable time-savers. For instance, when I need a broom, I go to the—" Shirley looked expectantly at her audience to finish the sentence.

"The broom closet!" someone called out. A burst of laughter swept through the group, as most of the women there knew there was no room for such a luxury in their homes.

"Well," Shirley went on with a smile. "I call mine a cleaning closet. When I need medicine, I go to the Sick Box, and I'll explain what that is later. When I need towels, I go to the linen closet; when I need an appliance warranty, I go to the filing cabinet.

"On your papers, you'll first see a description of my cleaning closet."

A Place for Everything

Cleaning Closet

Note: My cleaning closet is near the kitchen.

1. Has shelf with all cleaning supplies
2. Has nails for hanging
   a. mop
   b. broom
   c. dust pan
   d. wax applicator
   e. bag of vacuum cleaner bags
   f. bag of clean rags
3. Contains large items:
   a. vacuum cleaner
   b. floor polisher/waxer
   c. carpet sweeper
   d. broom
4. Has my Cleaning Caddy
   This plastic box with a handle can be purchased at a dime or discount store. In it I store the things I use every week to clean. I carry it with me from room to room—so I don't have to keep running back and forth for supplies:
   a. furniture polish
   b. dust rags
   c. glass cleaner
   d. 409 spray cleaner for fingerprints
   e. bathroom cleanser
   f. toilet disinfectant
   g. toilet brush
   h. feather duster
   i. whisk broom
   j. a fresh damp rag in a plastic bag (for wiping off what-nots)

Cleaning Caddy

Bathrooms

1. Under the sink:
   extra towels and washcloths
   one or two months' supply of
      toothpaste
      mouthwash
      soap
      deodorant
      toilet paper
      sponge and tub/tile cleaner for daily cleanups

   Note: I use a shoe box to store those small items. That way I can find things more easily and pick up the box to clean under it. If you have small children or visiting grandchildren, you will want to protect the closings so they cannot get in.

2. In a corner or a closet:
   A hamper—makes it easy to put away dirty clothes.

3. In an easily accessible place:
   A Sick Box—a cardboard or plastic box with medicines and first aid supplies, arranged in alphabetical order, with first-aid instructions handy.

4. In the medicine cabinet:
   All the other things that are bulging out of the medicine chest or lining your counter tops (razor and blades, deodorant, bath powder, makeup, contact-lens solution, aftershave, Q-tips, other grooming articles).

5. For bathing and showering items:
   Consolidate on a bathroom tray, shower caddy, or a shelf inside the tub

6. On inside of tub:
   A sponge and bottle of liquid detergent on side of tub so everyone can wipe up his/her own bathtub ring.

7. Additional towel racks:
   Use expandable wooden hat racks, or create racks by attaching to the bathroom wall two 1-foot panels, three feet apart, and connect with rods

Shirley reached over to the table, picked up a multicolored feather duster and large whisk broom and twirled them over her head. "I find these are grand things for my dusting and upholstery, especially when I'm in a hurry and don't want to take the time to get out my vacuum attachments. And it's great for lampshades, too! It almost makes me feel like a whirling dervish!"

"She really looks like one, too," Betty said, watching Shirley as she reached high and low, feather duster in one hand and whisk broom in the other.

"Now, in our imaginations, let's go to one of the bathrooms and talk about organizing it. You'll see that 'Bathrooms' comes next on our list. Most of us have a cabinet under the sink, so the ideas start there. (See p. 87.)

"You'll find that this system keeps your bathroom counters clear for something decorative and makes everything look spacious. It expedites cleaning, too."

Shirley took a few steps sideways, saying, "Now as we move on into the kitchen, let's stop a moment to look around. You know, a kitchen is probably the most personal part of our homes. We work there a great deal of the time, and most of us have specific ideas—ingrained in us by what our mothers had and did or didn't have and didn't do. We *know* how we want our kitchens to look.

"Personally, I like my kitchen counters clear. I don't want appliances or containers or anything else to clutter the broad sweep of my counters. Then I have space to work on anytime I want to cook or bake without having to shove something else out of the way. Maybe you prefer to have your appliances out within easy reach all the time—and that's fine. Whatever seems best for you! Remember, it's *your* kitchen!

"But what you should always ask yourself when you're getting ready to organize your kitchen is the question: Where is this item *First* going to be used? Is it going to be used *First* near the refrigerator, the sink, or the stove? Now we'll go through a system that works for me and can—perhaps with some revisions—work for you.

"Next is how to go about organizing your kitchen pantry." Shirley's eyebrows raised at the ripple of laughter that moved through the audience.

"Come, now," she said in mock severity, "don't you all have a shelf, or even several shelves, where you keep sup-

Kitchen

Principles for kitchen cabinets:

Place least-used items on the highest and lowest shelves.
Store items near the place of first use to eliminate wasted steps.

1. Place everyday dishes in the cabinet closest to the sink where you wash them or to the table, because that's where you usually use the dishes.

2. Place glasses near the sink. This is where you usually fill them so you're storing them according to the place where they'll first be used.

3. Keep everyday dishes and good china on separate shelves or in different cabinets.
   a. keep plates, bowls, saucers, cups, etc., together in neat stacks.
   b. keep serving bowls and platters together.

4. Use dividers (boxes or plastic organizers) in utensil drawers. Keep like-items together for easy accessibility (steak knives separate from place knives; large spoons from small ones, etc.).

5. Keep towels, dish cloths, and aprons in drawer near sink. (I find I get more into the drawer if I **roll** them.)

6. Reserve utility drawer (small) near stove for potholders, kitchen scissors, kitchen pliers, screwdriver, coupons, green stamps, etc. *Note:* That soon becomes a catch all. When in doubt, throw it out.

7. Use gadget drawer near stove for all small utensils such as strainer, masher, measuring spoons and cups, spatulas, melon scooper, potato peeler, etc.
   Note: **Eliminate everything from this drawer that is not absolutely essential for the way you cook.**

8. A peg board is handy, some women say, for hanging often-used gadgets and pans.

9. Utilize a drawer or shelves near the stove for foil, plastic wrap, baggies, etc.

10. Plastic containers and Tupperware also should go in one part of a cabinet handy to the sink, because that is where one usually fills them.

11. Arrange spices in alphabetical order on a small double turntable (a handy space-saver) in a cabinet near the stove (or use a spice rack).

12. Under the sink is a good place for a small garbage can, garbage bags, detergent, scouring powder and pads, etc.

13. Have a mixing center in your kitchen. Keep mixer (and/or food processor), measuring cups and spoons, and canisters here. Extra measuring cups and spoons in flour, rice, and sugar canisters save dishwashing during baking time.

14. Eliminate as many small appliances and as much clutter as possible from your counter tops. Cover remaining appliances with attractive matching covers.

plies—that extra can of whatever you got on sale, some things you don't *dare* run out of because you always use them in your cooking, things like that?"

As she looked at the affirmative nods and murmurs of assent, Shirley went on: "Well, those things need to be organized, too, so you know what you have and can get it out right away when you need it.

"I arrange my pantry by color. I have a red shelf, a green shelf and a yellow shelf, and so on. I also arrange my shelves by category. Beverages go together, as do spices and condiments, spreads, boxed items. Since most of us don't usually have either a lot of space or a lot of items, I suggest combining categories. But I label the shelf with masking tape, mostly so others can find things and know where to put things back. After using the shelves awhile, it becomes automatic to know where to look. The next chart (p. 91) gives some specific ideas that you may want to adopt.

"Now, after you've done all that, think a minute about one other place that needs organizing in our homes. That's the office, the *home* office. I find that it's vitally important for me to have a place that is my own for paper work. Many of my friends say they find it important, too.

"This home office can be merely a desk with a good light over it and a small filing cabinet. It can be made from a solid door, with two small filing cabinets—one at either end— holding it up.

"That's what I have. This is where I keep my pencils, paper, envelopes, stamps, address book. With a shelf above, it has become my study as well as my closet for private devotions, so it's where I keep all my Bibles and study books. Since my desk also serves in my home as a sewing-machine cabinet, I use the left-hand drawers for my sewing items and the right side for files.

"About those files—you know how it is when your husband isn't home and the freezer breaks down? Well, you can look up in the file to find if the compressor is still under warranty. My husband has delegated to me the responsibility

Organizing Pantry by Color

Shelf

1. Canned meats, fish and soups

2. Boxed dry items: macaroni, spaghetti, pancake mix, cornstarch, rice, flour, sugar, etc.

3. GREEN: green beans, peas, pickles, spinach

4. RED: tomato sauce, tomato paste, cherries, chili

5. ORANGE: peaches, yams, carrots

6. YELLOW: corn, pineapple, fruit cocktail

7. WHITE: applesauce, pears, canned milk, mushrooms

8. Beverages—coffee, tea, cocoa, fruit drinks

9. Spreads (peanut butter, jelly, syrup, honey, mustard—anything you *spread* on a sandwich)

10. Condiments and spices—salt, pepper, soy sauce, hot sauce, baking powder

11. Desserts—jello, puddings, cake mix, pie fillings

12. Dried fruits, nuts, snacks, and cereals

Notes: Many of these categories can be combined on *one shelf* if you want to make the best use of your space. For instance, items for shelves 8, 9, and 10 could be placed on different parts of one shelf. Or they could be stored on a shelf near the stove, if that is more convenient for you.

Label the shelf with masking tape so you'll remember which shelf is which color or category until you get used to the system.

for such household papers, so I keep them in my file. If your husband hasn't done so to you, then of course, these papers would be in *his* filing system. My files are in the top right-hand drawer of the filing cabinet at my desk. It has four sections: current, business/household papers, family records, and my study file.

"Obviously, my 'current' file contains folders with things I am working on or refer to often. There's a folder for bills; another for receipts; another for bankbooks and blank checks; one for correspondence; and another for current income-tax information.

"Just behind this 'current' section, I place the following file folders in alphabetical order: car papers; income-tax returns; insurance papers; investment papers; real-estate information; vacation references; warranties and instructions. These items pertain to long-standing business or household matters.

"The next section contains our family records. I have a large manila envelope for each person and write on the outside the information it contains. See, it looks like this.

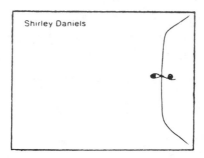

I find this section comes in very handy. For example, the school called the other day and asked for my husband's social-security number. I wondered how I would ever find that on the spur of the moment. I looked in the family file and there it was! I was able to find it quickly because each person's information is in a separate envelope.

"Last is the section for the things I'm studying—things that are special to me. When I'm studying a certain subject, I just slip it in that file according to the category under which it belongs. I keep mine topical, in alphabetical order. Currently, this file contains these subjects: Bible; Christian growth; discipleship; Holy Spirit; homemaking; marriage; party ideas; odds and ends.

"You'll notice that the next sheets give you in outline form what I've just said.

My Home Office

Desk with good light and a small filing cabinet containing:

Section A: Current Paper Work
1. Bills
2. Receipts (including separate small envelopes for receipts, receipts deductible, profits, auto repair slips, medical, etc.)
3. Bank books & blank checks
4. Correspondence (to be answered)
5. Current income tax information

Section B: Business/Household Records
1. Car papers
2. Income tax returns
    keep all tax records at least three years.
    keep income records at least six years (receipts, canceled checks and appraisals used to back up claims for IRS credits and deductions should be kept three years)
    keep all receipts for home improvement projects until you sell the house.
3. Insurance papers
4. Investment papers
5. Real estate (rental or mortgage papers)
6. Vacation references
7. Warranties and instructions

Notes: It's a good idea to write a "letter of location and instruction" for your family or executor of your will, in case you die or become disabled.

For records you want to keep a long time (home improvement receipts, etc.) I suggest using large envelopes or labeled storage boxes in a closet.

Wills can be kept in the lawyer's office, with a copy in your safe-deposit box or home record file.

I suggest putting things you might need in an emergency (will copy, passport, birth certificates, insurance policies, etc.) in a bank safe-deposit box.

Section C: Family Records (one envelope for each)
1. Our marriage certificate
2. Work resumes
3. Prescription for glasses
4. Immunization and other medical records
5. Passports (or keep in safe deposit box)
6. Discharge papers
7. College and high school diplomas
8. Other awards or recognitions
9. Birth certificate
10. Social Security record

Section D: My Study File
1. Bible
2. Christian Growth
3. Discipleship
4. Holy Spirit
5. Homemaking
6. Marriage
7. Party Ideas
8. Odds and Ends

"By the way, on the next page, you'll find a few 'cleaning recipes' that the women of our church have developed, and I think you'll find them useful and inexpensive.

"Well, it's almost time to end this session, but before we leave, I'd like to share one more principle of home management. You remember that we've talked about eliminating clutter, organizing what's left, having a place for everything; and a little bit about some clean-up hints. But don't forget what I call 'cleaning as you go.'

"That's right, *cleaning as you go*! This is a cardinal principle of home management. It means, first, that when you walk through a room, you try to leave it more orderly than it was. This simple principle saves lots of back-and-forth movements.

"Next, if you make a mess, try to clean it up before you go on to make another mess. For example, when I'm cooking, I find that if I just fix a big sink of hot soapy water and put my utensils in there as I use them, well, when there's a lull in the cooking, I can wash them all up or load some of them in the dishwasher. By the time the supper's on the table, the kitchen is pretty well cleaned up. At least things are soaking so they'll be easy to wash afterwards, whether by hand or machine.

"In our home, before we go to bed, we all help take everything we've brought into the family room for the evening— schoolbooks, sewing, drinks, shoes, whatever—back to wherever it came from or should go. With us all working together, it takes about ten minutes to put the snack dishes in the dishwasher, pick up the newspaper and other items, and generally remove the clutter.

"Then I check the bathrooms to make sure towels are up, and that is also where I sometimes collect things for the 'Displaced Items' box—but more about that another time!

"I just want to mention here that if you prepare for the morning rush the night before, it takes the hectic scramble—yes, and even the panic—out of the early morning. So the children lay out their clothes for the next day, lunches are

Five Fantastic Cleaning Recipes

Cleaning Recipe #1

For fingerprints and anything you would use 409 to clean
1 c. sudsy ammonia
1 pt. rubbing alcohol
1 T. liquid detergent
Put in gallon jug and fill with water.

Cleaning Recipe #2

For mirrors, bathroom fixtures, stainless steel—anything that needs a solvent (oven door, chrome toaster, etc.)
Spray with rubbing alcohol and rub dry.

Cleaning Recipe #3

For scarred and banged-up furniture
0000 steel wool
brown paste shoe polish
Liquid Gold furniture polish
Pour Liquid Gold into pad of steel wool. Smear that in can of paste polish and rub furniture with it. Let it stand twenty minutes. Then take soft cloth and go back over it. It heals the scars and makes the furniture look almost new. If there are spots of paint or any other discoloration, go back over again.

Cleaning Recipe #4

For removing stickers kids have stuck on doors
If the kids have put stickers on doors or furniture, peel off all you can with your fingers. Go back and put **peanut butter** on. Let stand for a couple of hours. Wipe off peanut butter and peel off all you can of remaining sticker with fingers or dull knife. Rub lightly with steel wool and the rest will come off. Now, go over with shoe polish treatment and surface will look brand new.

Cleaning Recipe #5

For removing old furniture wax or polish
1 tsp. Tide or Dreft
1 qt. warm water
Wring out a soft clean cloth in this solution and apply with the grain. Rinse with a cloth wrung out in clean warm water. Dry with a clean cloth. Work on a small area at a time. Apply new coat of wax or polish like Guardsman.

made the night before, and schoolwork and books are laid by the front door for a fast, uneventful exit.

"Remember, it takes twenty-one days for something to become a habit, so why not begin today? See you next week!"

11

Renae's Cleaning Spree

The morning after the fourth meeting with Shirley, Renae stood in the kitchen sipping ice-cold orange juice and staring at the table where she had carefully divided Shirley's directions into separate piles. Just thinking of what she ought to do gave her a sinking feeling.

Drumming her fingers on the kitchen counter, Renae became aware of the voices of the two girls that rose and fell in their bedroom down the hall.

She had been so proud of their daughters' room when she and Steve finished it. She loved its canopied beds, matching curtains, and round table covers. But none of it seemed to matter much to the girls. They just took it all for granted, strewing clothes, books, and food around with equal abandon.

The sounds from the girls' bedroom suddenly erupted, as a door banged open. Kathy burst into the kitchen. "Moth-*er*!" Kathy's voice rose stridently, her auburn curls bounced angrily. Her greenish-blue eyes, thick-lashed and usually dreamy with far-off goals, flashed with icy-cold lights.

"What is it now, Kathy?"

"That—that *dumb bunny*!" Kathy cried heatedly, unable to think of a more-allowable negative word in the stress of the moment. "She's—she's—"

Kathy's color was extremely heightened, and her chest was heaving with emotion. Renae was more concerned for her than for what the girl was saying. "Kathy, darling, whatever it is, you shouldn't let yourself get so angry."

"Mother," Kathy went on without paying attention to the interruption, "you promised you wouldn't let Melissa Jane wear my clothes anymore—and *you* did and *she* did—and now it's all spoiled!" Kathy rubbed her small, slightly upturned nose, just as she used to as a small child, and burst into angry tears.

The clothes were a problem, Renae knew, especially since Melissa had gotten to be the same size as her older sister. As Renae opened her mouth to call her second daughter, Melissa sauntered innocently into the kitchen and gave her mother a pussy-cat smile. Renae's heart went out to this child. Not nearly as pretty as her sister, Melissa made up for her dull brown hair and pale, artless face by her clever wit and intelligence.

A frown puckered Renae's forehead as she sighed. She recognized the cruel bent that Melissa's cleverness had taken on recently, especially with her older sister, but Renae didn't know what to do about it.

"Melissa," she asked sternly, "what is this all about?"

"Oh, I just borrowed one of Kathy's old blouses to wear to school." Melissa suppressed a little giggle.

"It wasn't an *old* blouse, and you know it!" Kathy interrupted, stopping her sobs for a moment. "It was my *new* blouse that I was saving to wear this weekend on my date with Allen. And it matched my red slacks. And you tore a hole in it!" Kathy sobbed more loudly than before.

"Not on purpose," Melissa defended herself. "And how was I to know that it was new and you were saving it?"

Kathy swung her head around at that and stared at Melissa. Incensed, she replied sharply, "It still had the tags on and you cut them off, that's how! You creep! I wish you weren't my sister!"

Melissa's face grew still and even paler, if that were possible.

Renae intervened, "Now, Kathy, you know you don't mean that; you shouldn't say it. I'll see that you get another blouse in time for your date. And Melissa, you are *not* to borrow Kathy's clothes without Kathy's permission. You apologize to her right now. Kathy, stop crying this minute. Melissa—"

"All right. I'm sorry," Melissa said through clenched teeth.

The two girls glowered at each other, Kathy mopping her eyes.

"Now, I have things for you both to do today and I want *no more fussing!* I want you girls to clean your closets and drawers."

"But, Mother—" both girls said at the same time.

"I'm not having any back talk from either of you. Here, Kathy, take this paper I got from my class; it will tell you how to do it. I'm going to clean the stove. Hurry now. We'll go out together for pizza in—four hours! Okay?"

As the girls turned unhappily to start their jobs, Renae said, "Wait. Hold on a minute. I forgot to give you these boxes and paper sack. Here, Melissa, take them."

"Whatever are they for?"

"Read the paper and you'll see!" was all the advice Renae gave, turning back to the stove.

She thought to herself, *I want to be able to see that I've changed. I want shiny counters, sparkling windows—and a proud feeling when I open the oven! Yes, and getting the girls to fix their own closets is making them take responsibility.*

She smiled at her virtuous self-justification, knowing how much she herself dreaded cleaning the closets, even with Shirley's helpful suggestions.

An hour later, after laying newspaper down on the floor— it had taken her at least ten minutes to find enough paper— Renae had warmed the oven and sprayed it. Since the spray was in the third place she looked, she had thought wistfully of Shirley's Cleaning Caddy. After coughing, and coughing, and more coughing, Renae went to see how the girls were getting along while the oven cleaner did its work.

The room was chaos. Clothes, books, games, shoes, and socks spilled out of closets and drawers. The boxes and paper bag were empty. The girls were looking at their baby pictures in an old album they had found.

Renae leaned weakly against the doorjamb and started to giggle. It was a little gurgle at first, just barely audible; but it soon became a river of laughter that had her bent double, hooting away. After a first startled look, the girls joined in, almost rolling on the floor.

Then, as suddenly as it had started, the storm of laughter was over. Renae looked around soberly at the mess and said, "Let's get out of here. We'll take an early break and when we come back, we'll be ready to tackle it in order like the paper says—and get it done. We'll just close the door to your room for now."

12

From Chaos to Order

Rain had been falling for hours. It had filled up the low place in the back yard and still whispered against the windows. An occasional lightning flash, followed by a rumble of thunder, reminded Renae that summer was really on the way.

It was an effort to get ready for Shirley's class, but of course she did. For one thing, it would have been embarrassing to try to find a reasonable explanation to give to Betty for not coming with her. Besides, with the encouragement she was getting from Steve, she knew she wanted to keep on with a good thing.

With a sigh, Renae slipped into her seat. She couldn't believe she hadn't brought her umbrella, even though Betty had picked her up in the garage. Now she was wet and the air-conditioning was cold—and she felt disagreeable! Frowning, she thought back over the weekend.

Things hadn't really gone the way she had expected: it all took so long! But the oven did get clean. And the girls' closets and drawers *finally* were put back in order as the three of them meticulously followed Shirley's papers on "Arranging Closets and Drawers."

It had all seemed worthwhile when Steve's pleased smile had curved his lips and crinkled the corners of his vividly blue eyes.

But now Renae was tired and wet. She just sat, glad to be sitting down quietly, glad the chair was there to hold her up, glad not to have to be *doing* anything.

Renae's shoulders drooped as she remembered noticing the messy desk this morning on her way out of the house. Discouraged at the thought of all the things she had *not* done, she looked around, wondering if anyone else felt like she did.

When Shirley moved to the front, Renae tried to look interested but thought, *A clean oven and one beautifully arranged closet hardly seem significant.* "Twenty-one days to change your lifestyle." That's what Shirley had said, Renae remembered. Twenty-one days!

Idly, Renae wondered if she would be able to survive those three vital weeks of change. And even if she really wanted to. Hearing again Steve's soft chuckle and picturing the corners of his mouth lifted into that smile, she was reminded that making this organization thing work was important to her marriage, her home, and to herself.

"How would you describe yourself right now?" Shirley asked as she began the class. "Other than 'wet,' I mean. Discouraged? Despairing? Defeated? Or maybe things went well for you last week, as you tried to move into new areas in your home management. From here, I can just about tell which is which—by looking at your faces!

"That's okay. Even if nothing went right this last week, even if you weren't able to accomplish anything at all in your attempt to change your home management, the fact that you are back here this morning means that you're still in there, trying. And that's good!

"You may not have your home all organized yet—" Shirley waited for the laughter to subside and then continued, "—and I know you'll keep thinking of new ways to organize your house. I do! So today we won't add to that list. Instead, we'll be going into ways of organizing our housework.

"But first, I'd like us to consider again the reason behind getting our lives in order. Remember that old formula we learned back in school about telling things properly? You've got to get in all the facts: WHO?—WHY?—WHAT?—WHEN?—and WHERE?

"We know most of the answers. The *who* is 'us.' The *what* is 'managing home priorities.' The *when* is what we're working on in our 'schedules.' The *where*, of course, is 'our homes'—and 'our lives.'

"Those items were easy to figure out. So now, let's take an in-depth look at the *why*'s.

"First, for me, is that God the Father is orderly. You have only to look at his creation to realize that! His world is orderly and organized: day and night, season following season, planting and harvest, sowing and reaping.

"God also tells us that things don't just happen by chance or haphazardly. He has plans for everything, and that includes us. Look at Psalm 33:11: 'But the plans of the LORD stand firm forever, the purposes of his heart through all generations [NIV].'

"David exulted in Psalm 40:5:

> Many, O LORD my God,
>   are the wonders you have done.
> The things you planned for us
>   no one can recount to you;
> were I to speak and tell of them,
>   they would be too many to recount [NIV].

"And in Jeremiah 29:11, we read:

'For I know the plans I have for you,' declares the LORD, 'plans to prosper you and not to harm you, plans to give you hope and a future [NIV].'

"Micah's indictment against his people was: 'But they do not know the thoughts of the LORD; they do not understand his plan . . . [4:12, NIV].'

"I want to know the thoughts of the Lord," Shirley continued. "I want to understand God's plans for my life. And I know you do, too.

"Dr. Charles Stanley, pastor of the First Baptist Church of Atlanta, recently said some exciting things about the apostle Paul and God's plans for him. I think Paul can be an example to us today. Paul had planned his itinerary and had written to the church in Corinth about it in First Corinthians 16:5–8:

> After I go through Macedonia, I will come to you—for I will be going through Macedonia. Perhaps I will stay with you awhile, or even spend the winter, so that you can help me on my journey, wherever I go. . . . But I will stay on at Ephesus until Pentecost . . . [NIV].

"Dr. Stanley comments about Paul's schedule:

> It sounds like Paul is uncertain. That is true. He was uncertain.
>
> He was uncertain in the sense that though he planned, he was willing and, I believe, eager to submit to God's schedule daily.
>
> On the face of it, you may think it inconsistent to plan ahead and still be totally flexible to changes which God wants in your life. How else can you expect to obey God? That is the only way you can walk with the Lord.
>
> Here is what I mean:

Lord, You have permission at any moment,
   regardless of what my plans are,
You have permission at any moment to change my course
   in the middle of the stream—
   at any moment.
I am available for Your change.

    What we must do is trust in the wisdom and sovereignty of
God since it is His schedule, and my life is His.

    "That was so encouraging for me to hear—and it ties right
in with Psalm 37:23 (in the King James Version): *'The steps
of a good man are ordered by the LORD. . . .'*
    "Another of God's promises in this regard is found in
Psalm 32:8 to 10. The New International Version reads:

I will instruct you and teach you in the way you should go; I
will counsel you and watch over you. Do not be like the horse
or the mule, which have no understanding, but must be con-
trolled by bit and bridle or they will not come to you. . . . the
LORD's unfailing love surrounds the man who trusts in him.

    "Paul tells us in First Corinthians 14:40 that God expects
us to do things in the same way God himself does. 'In a
fitting and orderly way,' says the New International Version.
The King James Version says, 'decently and in order.' The
New American Standard translates this 'properly and in an
orderly manner.' I guess we get the idea.
    "Jesus tells us that it is God's plan for our lives that we
bear fruit. And he goes on to add, 'much fruit.' And, as if that
isn't strong enough, Jesus describes it as 'fruit that will last.'
    "This fruit is defined for us in Galatians 5:22 and 23 as
'the fruit of the Spirit.' Remember that Jesus called himself
the Vine and told us that we are the branches upon which he
intends to bear fruit."
    As she talked, Shirley rotated the big blackboard to show a
drawing of a vine trunk and a branch, which she labeled
CHRIST and US. She quickly sketched in a luscious-looking

bunch of grapes and wrote boldly on it the word LOVE. With a swirl of her short full skirt, Shirley turned back to her audience. Pausing for emphasis, she said, "The fruit of the Spirit—is—LOVE:

JOY is love smiling.

PEACE is love resting.

PATIENCE is love waiting.

KINDNESS is love showing itself sensitive to the needs of others.

GOODNESS is love making allowances and sacrifices for others.

FAITHFULNESS is love proving constant.

GENTLENESS is love yielding.

SELF-CONTROL is love triumphing over selfish inclinations."

There was a sudden quiet in the room. No one moved, as each woman was absorbed in her own thoughts.

Renae pushed her glasses up on her nose. What Shirley had just said opened a whole new concept of love. She thought briefly of the girls and of Steve. And of God. These classes were showing her a whole different set of values.

She felt a thrill of discovery, thinking, *God is wonderful and important! His plan for my life seems to be consistent, orderly, and designed to make me more like Jesus.* Renae realized that she had been so overwhelmed by all the details of living that she hadn't thought much about the design of her life—or the Designer.

Shirley's voice broke into her reflection. She was praying:

Father, thank you for challenging us with love, *your* love. Thank you for letting us see that you had a plan when you designed the universe. That you created things in a consistent order—the latter dependent on the former. That you dislike things to be disorderly and upset; that you like harmony.

Thank you for showing us that part of our obedience to you is being sure everything is done properly and in an orderly manner. Thank you for making plain again how far short we fall of your intentions for us.

And as we consider today our home priorities, help us to see that if we are organized, we are free to do all you want us to do. Show us again that your world is orderly and organized: day and night, seasons, planting and harvest, sowing and reaping.

Help us to be like you in all we do. Help us to bear the fruit of your Spirit by abiding in Jesus. Thank you. Amen.

There was a general shuffling as Shirley finished her prayer. Renae felt a drop of rainwater slide down the back of her neck and shivered.

"If I asked you quickly to name six things that you have to do every morning, could you?" Shirley asked, staccato fashion.

"Probably so," she answered herself. "We all have to get up, fix breakfast, get husband and kids off, and so on. But what I'm talking about is *after* all that! You know, after everyone's left and you can sit quietly and have a cup of coffee before you begin the day's activities!

"What are they—those *'day's activities'*? Do you know? Well, today's set of papers is titled prosaically, 'Organizing Your Housework.' Hopefully, there will be something that will help each of us. These sheets include suggestions for housework activities, menu planning, and your personal planning notebook. As you see, we start with what I was just talking about—a list of household activities. This is actually a repeat of a form you already have—previously titled 'Scheduling Your Homemaking,' but we need to take another look."

"In my personal schedule, I've discovered that *an ounce of morning is worth a pound of afternoon*! So I've established 'Six Imperatives for the Morning.' These are specific jobs and

108

schedules that I follow each day. As we check them out together, you may find them helpful in structuring a day that will enhance your family life and be equally pleasing to God.

Six Imperatives for the Morning

1. Start dinner preparation (to prevent panic at 4:30!).
   For example, if meat is frozen, take out to thaw. Make gelatin salad or put together a casserole.
2. Wash breakfast dishes (while you are still in the kitchen).
3. Get dressed. It's very difficult to clean house in a clumsy robe.
4. Make the beds. (Children should make their own beds and tidy their rooms, if old enough).
5. Straighten the house.
   Walk through each room, putting items into place.
   Carry a laundry basket or a box to deposit misplaced items as you walk through the house; then place them where they belong when you come to that room.
   Toys or clothes left lying around by the children go into the "displaced box" mentioned earlier.
6. Clean bathroom fixtures when needed.

"Remember, the Living Bible's paraphrase of Proverbs 16:9 is 'We should make plans—counting on God to direct us.'

"That's my routine. I do these six things before starting any other projects. In this way, my house is straight by nine or nine-thirty, whether it's clean or not, dinner preparation is begun, and I'm free to begin the rest of the day's activities. I can leave the house if I have to, feeling that things are under control.

"Most of us are helped by doing specific jobs on specific days, which is why we were working on scheduling our activities—to know *what* we need to do and *when* it best fits our schedule to do it. I've listed the housework that most books and magazines consider *weekly* jobs. As we read them together, you will need to decide which day you will do each thing.

List of Household Activities

Daily

1. Beds
2. Clutter picked up
3. Dishes washed and kitchen clean
4. Bathrooms
5. Meal preparation

Weekly or Every Other Week

1. Vacuum
2. Mop
3. Dust and polish furniture
4. Shopping and errands
5. Change bed linen
6. Clean stove and refrigerator (day before shopping)
7. Laundry
8. Menu planning
9. Baking
10. Sewing (or hobby)

Periodically

1. Wash curtains
2. Clean windows/woodwork
3. Clean out closets/drawers
4. Shampoo carpets
5. Polish silver
6. Put away out-of-season clothes

"On the next page of the stapled sheets, you will see my own housework schedule. It shows where and how I plan my time. This is what I suggested earlier that *you* do with the 'Specific Weekly Tasks' list. Please don't think that I'm advocating that you have to do everything exactly as I say and do. It's just my prayer that you'll discover some secrets of organization that will help you."

Specific Weekly Tasks

1. Clean house thoroughly and keep house picked up and neat.
2. Wash clothes and mend.
3. Plan menus and grocery-shop.
4. Do major monthly cleaning jobs (any day, any week, just so they all get done).
   - clean oven
   - clean range
   - mop and wax floors
   - clean refrigerator
   - clean mildew from shower stalls, etc.
   - clean baseboards and ledges
   - wash blankets and scatter rugs
   - clean outside surfaces of cabinets
   - clean closets, cupboards, drawers as needed
5. Shop and run errands.
6. Sew.
7. Bake.
8. Do quarterly and semi-annual cleaning jobs.
9. Other

"I guess what I'm trying to say is that the most important thing is to *have* a housework schedule and to *follow* it. Plan your own schedule to fit your personal needs and inclinations.

"There are two other kinds of cleaning that we will be considering later on: *quarterly cleaning* and *semi-annual cleaning*, usually done in spring and fall. I've included them here with this set of papers, so that all the housework projects would be together. As you can see, these, too, fit into my schedule.

Shirley, head cocked characteristically on one side, looked expectantly at the faces before her. No one spoke. The women seemed numbed, so she continued: "Some of my friends use a card-file system—rather than the outline

My Housework Schedule

Daily

Six Imperatives for the Morning
1. Start dinner preparation
2. Wash breakfast dishes
3. Get dressed
4. Make the beds
5. Straighten house
6. Clean bathroom fixtures when needed

Weekly

Mondays
1. Change linen on beds
2. Wash clothes and fold
3. Mend
4. Dust furniture
5. Vacuum where necessary

Tuesdays
1. Church meetings and ministry to others
2. Errands and shopping

Wednesdays
BIG CLEANING PROJECTS
Mornings
1st Wed. of month: Clean oven and range
2nd Wed. of month: Clean refrigerator and outside surfaces of cabinets
3rd Wed. of month: Mop and wax kitchen floors and clean shower stall
4th Wed. of month: Clean baseboards and ledges, wash scatter rugs, blankets, etc.
5th Wed. of month: Clean any closets, cupboards, and drawers necessary
Afternoons
Time for self or appointments, sewing, studying, hobby, etc.

Thursdays
CLEAN HOUSE THOROUGHLY
1. Mop kitchen and bathrooms
2. Dust furniture
3. Clean mirrors and glass tables
4. Wipe off what-nots with a damp cloth
5. Vacuum carpet and upholstered furniture
6. Clean bathrooms
7. Water plants

Fridays
1. Plan menus (or do this Thursday afternoons)
2. Shop for groceries and run errands
3. Prepare for dinner guests, if any

Saturdays
Mornings
1. Wash a load of clothes and fold
2. Bake

3. Sunday-dinner preparation
   make dessert
   prepare vegetables
   prepare congealed salad
   wrap baked potatoes
   cut up chicken or make casserole
   set table
   make iced tea
      Afternoons and Evenings
Family time

Sundays

1. Church
2. Ministry
3. Rest
4. Family time

schedule that I use and Scotch-tape to one of my kitchen cabinet doors.

"These women took the list of homemaking activities— one of the sheets from our third class—and each one customized it to fit her lifestyle, making additions or deletions as necessary. Then she copied each activity onto a three by five card and filed it under 'Daily' or the particular day of the week she scheduled it.

"The principle is the same, whichever way you decide is best for you. What it means to me is that they have a 'vertical file' in a file box, and I have a 'horizontal file' on a piece of paper. It's your choice.

Quarterly Cleaning Projects

Saturday, first month
Polish furniture (once a year, I remove old wax and apply new.)
Saturday, second month
Sort seasonal clothing
Saturday, third month
Polish silver
Saturday, fourth month
Wash windows (a school-age child can wash his/her own bedroom windows).

Semi-Annual Cleaning Projects

Clean draperies
Wash and iron curtains
Shampoo carpets
Clean walls
Rearrange furniture
Wax floors
Make any necessary repairs
   Note: I find that if I attempt only one room at a time and spend a day to a week on it (depending on Its size), I can keep up with the meals, wash, and do light routine cleaning of the rest of the house. The average house can be thoroughly cleaned this way over a month's time.

"One of the most valuable timesavers I've discovered in homemaking is weekly menu planning. It is very simple and takes only one hour a week to do, but it conserves countless time, money, and energy. I find I'm more likely to prepare a balanced meal if it is planned in advance. You'll find all this in the next set of sheets stapled together. I'll share some shortcuts I've found.

"First, breakfast menus. I plan them only one time and repeat them weekly for as long as I want. I post this menu on the inside of one of my kitchen cabinet doors for easy reference. You'll see that I've included some sample breakfast menus in your papers. If you get bored with their predictability or want to take advantage of seasonal fruits, you can revise the plan periodically.

"You'll notice that I put an asterisk after French Cheese Puff. This is our family tradition on Christmas morning. It's nice because it's easy on Mom. Your family may enjoy it, too, so I've included the recipe.

"Well, as you can see, that takes care of breakfasts for our family. You might want to do that first, although your breakfast plans may be the same or different from ours.

"Second, notice on my weekly schedule that I plan my dinner menus on Friday morning, because I shop on Friday, but it could be done on Thursday afternoon.

Easy Breakfast Menus

Sunday
Orange juice
Cinnamon rolls
Cereal with milk
Coffee/milk

Monday
Orange juice
Scrambled eggs
Grits
Bacon (optional)
Toast
Coffee/milk

Tuesday
Grapefruit half
Pancakes (mix) OR
Waffles (frozen)
Syrup
Coffee/milk

Wednesday
Orange juice
Stewed prunes
3-minute boiled eggs
Biscuits
Butter and jelly
Coffee/milk

Thursday
Grapefruit half
Cooked cereal (oatmeal, etc.)
Milk
Toast
Cocoa/coffee

Friday
Orange juice
French toast (a good way to use
    stale bread)
Syrup
Bacon (optional)
Coffee

Special Occasion Breakfast
Canteloupe slices
French Cheese Puff*
Cinnamon loaf (warmed and
    buttered)
Sausage patties
Coffee/milk

*FRENCH CHEESE PUFF RECIPE

Overnight in refrigerator   Oven: 350° F.

16 slices white bread
Butter or margarine
1 package sliced Cheddar or
    American cheese (8 slices)

6 eggs, well beaten
1 quart milk
1 tsp. salt
¼ tsp. pepper

Combine eggs, milk, and seasonings. Remove crusts and butter each slice of bread. Place bread and cheese in buttered 9x13" pan, sandwich-style. Pour egg-milk mixture over bread and refrigerate overnight. Set 9x13" pan in larger pan containing hot water. Bake about one hour at 350° F. Ready when knife comes out clean. Cut in squares and garnish with dollops of red jelly. Serves 8-10.

For half recipe, use 8x8" pan; bake about 30 minutes.

My Recipe File

My key to speedy planning
Quickly get ideas for a main dish, then pull out the cards for a salad, vegetable, and simple dessert to finish out the meal.

Recipes
1. On 5" x 8" index cards
2. Include conventional and microwave-cooking directions
3. If it's a main dish, I include mention of a salad, vegetable, and dessert that would go well with it to make a meal

File has three dividers
1. *Family-Tested Recipes:* for everyday meals
2. *Special-Occasion Recipes:* fancy recipes for appetizers, luncheons, and gastronomical fantasies
3. *Guest Menus:* a card file of guests (alphabetized by last name) and the menu I served them, with the date

---

"To plan, I sit down down with Thursday's newspaper food ads, my recipe file, and my grocery list—already partially filled out with items I need, mainly staples or cleaning products that need replenishing. The next page of your stapled sheets outlines my recipe file—my key to speedy planning.

"As you see, this is not the ordinary run-of-the-mill recipe file. It is different in that it contains three sections. My family-tested recipes are used for everyday meals. Fancy recipes for appetizers, luncheons, and gastronomical fantasies are reserved for a special-occasion section, as is my guest file.

"I write my recipes on five by eight index cards and include both conventional and microwave cooking directions. Also, if it's a main dish, including notes about a salad, vegetable, and dessert that would go well with it makes it easy to plan the whole meal. The beauty of this file is that I can quickly get ideas for a main dish, then pull the cards for the salad, vegetable, and simple dessert to finish out the meal.

"The grocery ads let me know what is on sale. If chicken is on special that week, I know to pull out at least one chicken

My Grocery List Guide

Note: I make a sheet on Monday and keep it by the toaster to add to all
week. Then I complete it before going to the store, after planning my
menus.

Juices	*Dairy*	*Canned*
	Eggs	
	Cheese	
	Milk	

Staples and Boxed Goods	*Bottled*
Rice	Catsup
Sugar	Syrup
Flour	Cokes
Salt	
Cocoa	
Cereals	
Crackers	

Cleaning Supplies

Breads   *Frozen Goods*

Meats   *Fresh Fruits and Vegetables*

recipe from the file to use in my menu planning for the
upcoming week. Proverbs 12:27b fits into this very well, I
think. As the Living Bible puts it: 'The diligent man makes
good use of everything he finds.'

"After I write down my menus, I complete my grocery list
by including the required ingredients. I also check the pantry
to see what sale items I can use and what staple items I'm
out of that I may have forgotten to put on my list during the
previous few days.

"On the next sheet, you'll find 'My Grocery List Guide.' It
might be helpful to you, too. You may notice I've made it out
according to the layout of the grocery store where I shop
most often. I also sort my rebate coupons in the same order.

"Now I can arrive at the grocery store armed with my grocery list, store coupons, a week's menu—*and blinders to everything I don't need!*" Laughter swept the room; everyone knew exactly what Shirley meant.

Then Shirley went on, "Let's look now at one of the last items in this set of stapled sheets. It's called 'My Personal Planning Book.' I have found that a wonderful time-planning tool for me as a busy homemaker is a personal notebook that fits in my purse. In it I record appointments, birthdays, lists of things to do and buy, and special projects I wish to accomplish during the month. The alphabetical section at the back keeps addresses and phone numbers at my fingertips.

"The notebook I use is a 3¼" x 5" six-ring binder from Star Diary System, Success Mail Service, P.O. Box 15507, Santa Ana, California 92705. It's a looseleaf book with pages dated for each day of the month.

"The important thing about a personal notebook is that you have it with you at all times. Whenever and wherever you think of something you need to do, to buy, or to remember, you can jot it down immediately in your purse notebook on the day you intend to do it.

"Two other items that have proven their worth in our household are kept right by the telephone in the kitchen. The first is our family's monthly calendar. Now that our children are older, each person is expected to mark on the calendar the events during that month that are of special importance to him or her. Then the rest of us know how we can fit into each other's schedules and nothing is left out or forgotten.

"The second is 'Our Telephone Message Book.' This is simply a dated stenographer's pad on which all telephone messages for someone in the household are recorded. Each person can then check for calls upon arriving home. That way no important call or phone number is unreported.

"I'd like to state again emphatically that I am in no way advocating that you do everything exactly as I do it. I have in no way arrived at where I want to be. I am still in the process

My Personal Planning Notebook

1. Each day I make a "To Do" list, including items that are regularly sched-uled for that day, like clean house, grocery shop, meetings, etc. I also include other things that need to be done, for example: pick up suit from cleaners, dental appointment, 3:30, call Beth Jones, make dessert for S.S. meeting.

2. Then I number the items in the order they need to be done, beginning with number one and work down the list, checking off items as they are accomplished. If some items don't get done, I transfer them to the next day's list. I quoted this verse earlier, but it fits here, too, and is good for us to remember.
   We should make plans,
   counting on God to direct us. (Proverbs 16:9, TLB).
   I pray over my plans and give the Lord permission to change them. Often he does—with divine "interruptions"—but I always accomplish more with a written plan than with one that is only in my head.

   c. The monthly calendar section follows the daily section. It is ideal for recording future appointments, birthdays, and coming events.

   d. The cash section is used to record expenses.

   e. The notes section provides extra paper for taking notes in church, or listing ideas, or leaving notes when visiting.
   I keep a "To Buy" list in my notebook, so that when I'm in a store I can always check to see if they have what I need. This is where I list clothes sizes for my husband, children, family, etc.

   I also list "Projects for the Month" that I'd like to accomplish.

   At the top of the daily page, I list "Prayer Requests" as people give them to me, so I will remember when I look at that particular day. Example: "Thursday, May 3—pray for Ann's surgery."

of becoming what God wants me to be—like his Son Jesus Christ. I still don't have it all together.

"Some of you are not ready to follow all these suggestions yet, but don't worry about that. Keep the sheets; when you're ready, you'll have some reference papers.

"I've had women call me a week or two after a seminar to get more information. In fact, yesterday morning I got a call from Marie, a woman I hadn't seen in some time. She told me that she was moving to a larger house and asked me to

---

The Monthly Family Calendar

Each person marks on the calendar the events during that month that are of special importance to him/her.

Our Telephone Message Book

A dated stenographer's pad on which all telephone messages for someone in the household are recorded.

---

send her the sheets on organizing a pantry. She had never had room for one before and was excited to be able to do it now.

"It is my earnest prayer that you'll discover some ideas and secrets of organization as I've shared with you—and that, because of our time together, *all* your life will be more pleasing to God, to your family, and to yourself.

"I'd like to close today with a verse I've found helpful. It's Colossians 3:16 and 17 from the New International Version."

Let the word of Christ dwell in you richly as you teach and admonish one another with all wisdom, and as you sing psalms, hymns and spiritual songs with gratitude in your hearts to God.

13

Renae Learns About Flexible Planning

Blinking in the bright sunlight, Renae pushed her sunglasses up on her nose. She lifted her feet gingerly, the sand scalding her insteps, as she followed the girls and Steve. The four girls—Kathy and Melissa and one friend each—were already down at the water's edge, hopping about and running in and out of the ocean.

"A *whole day* just for the family!" she had gloated at breakfast, ignoring the troubled glance Steve had shot her. He had merely touched her cheek with his warm hand and then she had gone on gaily prattling about her plans for the day. Now she wondered what he had been about to say.

The girls shrieked with glee, diving into the curling breakers. Her beach chair was waiting for her where Steve had set it up above the waterline. An odd sensation came over her; it felt almost as though she was going to step into a picture and make it complete. The children romping in the sparkling water, the man who stood at the edge watching them—they needed *her* to fill it out, even though none of them had yet recognized it.

She sat down, slipped her feet out of her sandals, and leaned back. As she watched, Kathy and her friend, swimming hard, reached the black rocks that acted as a sort of breakwater. They stood up, waving triumphantly. She waved back.

Steve turned then and came to her, sinking to his knees beside her chair. "Renae," he began hesitantly, "I—I don't know how to tell you this, exactly, but—"

"My mother always told me to get it over with and say it right out," she said as the pause lengthened.

"Well, we're going to have to go back early. I have a business meeting this afternoon I couldn't get out of, but—we'll have all morning and lunch together!"

"Oh, Steve! The whole day's spoiled!" The words were out before she could stop them. She knew her voice sounded harsh and ungracious, but added, "Why couldn't you at least have asked me? Or—or *warned* me?"

"I tried to, honey." Steve's face was miserable. "But there didn't seem to be a right time." His voice trailed off and his hand reached out tentatively.

She jerked away, angrily turning her back and looking out at an ocean blurred by tears. How long she sat there feeling sorry for herself she didn't know. But in time a thought surfaced in her mind, something Shirley had said.

Like a spoiled child, she'd been blaming Steve—and the men he had an appointment with—and even God!—for not letting her have the family day she wanted. And all the time God was trying to remind her that he had a plan and a schedule for her life.

"God," cried Renae, hearing the shouts of the children happily playing, seeing the gulls swooping and dipping over the waters, "how could you have done this to me? How could you have ordered this for today? I've just learned about the kind of wife and mother you want me to be—and I'm trying so hard. I didn't know about it or care about it for all those years, and now I really want to make Steve happy, to meet his needs.

"I want our family to be *your* kind of family. But how can that be, when this kind of thing happens the very first time I plan something special?"

A cloud of sand spewed over Renae as Melissa and Peggy slid to a stop beside her chair. "Hey, Mom, we're thirsty. Can we have something to drink?"

"There's some apple juice bags in the cooler. Help yourself—and be sure to put the lid back on tightly!" she called as the girls ran gaily off toward the red and white thermos box.

Suddenly Renae remembered that Shirley had been in a similar situation. There were some plans that were spoiled, and God had shown Shirley a verse. Renae had memorized it because it seemed so right: *The steps of a good man are ordered by the Lord.*

"Lord, you just don't want me to indulge in self-pity, do you?" She asked the question, even though she already knew the answer. A month or so ago, she would not have believed how much it helped to tell him everything she was thinking and feeling. Now she had a feeling he was answering her: "Renae, did you mean it this morning when you asked me to guide and direct you?"

"Why, of course, Lord."

"If you meant it, child, why are you fretting and complaining about what I brought into your life?"

"I'm sorry, Father. I know Shirley told us that when we ask you for guidance, you expect us to plan with flexibility, so we can obey you when you change our plans. And I really did mean it. I guess I just didn't know that you were going to change this day in mid-stream. And I *do* want what you want for me. Thank you for loving me enough to guide me."

Steve was slowly walking down the beach, his shoulders slumped. Renae smiled, remembering when Shirley had said that God does not direct our schedule to make it easy for us, but that our schedules are set by him to accomplish his purpose for our lives and for the lives of others we touch.

"That's what I want, Father—*your* purpose!" she whispered, running to meet Steve.

She took his hand. "I'm sorry I acted like a spoiled brat, darling. We have all the rest of the morning left. Let's take a dip!"

Steve smiled. "It's all right, Renae. We'll plan more family days. Beat you into the water!"

14

Systemizing Cleaning Procedures

This is the last session of the seminar," Shirley said with a smile as she faced the women. "And I want to thank each one of you for coming, for sticking it out, and for the feedback you have given me after the meetings.

"It is my prayer that our time together has shown you that managing your home priorities *frees* you to do the most important things in your busy life of trying to balance time for God, for family and homemaking, for job, ministry, volunteer work, leisure activities—and yourself.

"It's easy to come away from a day, a week—or even a year—with the sense that there wasn't a chance to do what we really wanted. Knowing your purpose in life and what your priorities are should free you from that kind of frustration. I hope you'll never again have that sinking feeling that the whole thing is going to be out of control all over again tomorrow. That's where your schedule and the homemaking and housecleaning tips will be helpful.

"And, most importantly, you know that if you do *all* the things you should *when* you should, you'll be free to do the other things you would like to do in reaching out to other people. Thanks again for joining me in the seminar. It's been fun for me and, I hope, helpful for you."

There was a murmur of consent, with a voice here and there saying, "We thank *you*, Shirley."

"I promised you cleaning procedures before we finished today. The sheets being distributed now have plans for weekly and monthly projects, spring-and-fall cleaning, a ten-minute emergency clean-up, ideas for catching up when you're behind, some tips for making cleaning easier, and some ideas on teaching your children how to help.

"If all this organizing and scheduling and listing sounds dreary to you, remember that *order is not an end in itself.* Order is whatever helps you function effectively. It is the means to your goal. The purpose of order in our lives—as Christian women, wives, and mothers—is provision and comfort for our families and being pleasing to God in all things.

"I try to clean my house thoroughly once a week. I find that doing it all in one day—or on two consecutive mornings—gives me a feeling of accomplishment. To see everything clean and shining at the same time brings joy to my heart. And so, more practically, it frees the other days of the week for other things.

"Let's take a quick look at the pages for today. You can study them more fully at home. First, is 'The Very Thorough Weekly Clean-Up.'

"As we all know, in addition to the very thorough *weekly* cleaning, there are certain things that have to be done occasionally—say, once a month. I do these on a day other than my regular weekly cleaning day. And I do one each week to keep from getting behind on those big jobs. The next chart

The Very Thorough Weekly Clean-Up

1. Do the **Six Imperatives for the Morning,** so the house is straightened up before you attempt to clean it!

2. Mop all floors that require mopping (usually kitchen and bathrooms). Personally, I find **Pine Sol,** diluted according to instructions, to be excellent **except** for no-wax vinyl floors. For them, I use a light detergent and water and rinse well.

3. Clean one room at a time—and proceed through all rooms.

   Note: Carry Cleaning Caddy containing supplies as you go from room to room. Do the following in each room:

   a. Vacuum upholstery or brush with whisk broom. Shake out draperies.
   b. Dust lamp shades with whisk broom or soft paint brush.
   c. Dust ornate picture frames, artificial flowers, and hard-to-reach surfaces with a feather duster.
   d. Dust wood furniture with old undershirt or cheesecloth. If you put down a good coat of wax (I like Guardsman) two or three times a year, you need only dust to bring up the shine. Rub hard to remove fingerprints. **Note:** Spray polishes leave a silicone build-up, so don't use on *wood* furniture.
   For plastic or Formica-finished furniture, I use a polish such as Pledge. Polish with a soft cloth.
   e. With a damp cloth wrung out in mild detergent, wipe off what-nots, vases, telephones, and tile windowsills.
   f. Clean mirrors with Windex or alcohol (Cleaning Recipe #2).
   g. Clean fingerprints from walls with Cleaning Recipe #1 or 409 Spray Cleaner.
   h. Vacuum carpets throughout the house after all the rooms have been cleaned. *Note:* If there's a wood floor, first vacuum the rug; then do the floor with the floor-brush attachment.

4. Clean bathrooms thoroughly.
   a. Put Pine Sol or Lysol in commode. Swish around with toilet brush.
   b. Wipe off outside of commode and seat with sponge squeezed out in Pine Sol.
   c. Clean sinks and tub with sponge and bathroom tub-and-tile cleaner. Shine with an old towel. Spray old fixtures with alcohol for sparkle.
   For removing tile film: If film remains on tile walls after cleaning with household cleaner, rub the dry walls with a piece of dry 000 steel wool without soap. The film will come off dry tile like talcum powder. Then go over tile with damp rag and household cleaner.
   To clean mildew from the shower stall, fill a spray bottle with household bleach. Spray shower tile and floor. Let dry. Rinse thoroughly by letting shower run a few minutes.
   Note: Be sure there is plenty of ventilation in the room when you use bleach. *Do not mix cleaning compounds.*
   d. Wipe off what-nots and tile window sills with damp rag.

e. Dust pictures, artificial flowers, and shelves with feather duster.
f. Clean mirrors with alcohol or Windex.
g. Remove fingerprints from walls with Cleaning Recipe #1 or 409.
h. Put out fresh towels and soap.

outlines my checklist for those monthly jobs, which are itemized on 'My Household Schedule' for Wednesdays.

"Next, I keep up with the cleaning jobs that need to be done quarterly by doing them on Saturday, although another day could be chosen. You can use my checklist as a guide when you plan your schedules.

"And then there's spring and fall cleaning, in a class all by themselves! The next sheet is to serve as a reminder—or checklist, if you will—for those things we need to do semi-annually.

"Then there are always times when we get behind and are unprepared to have guests. The kids are sick, *we* are sick, or any number of things could happen! And in the midst of all the mess, we get a phone call that someone is coming to visit. That's when the next two checklists will come in handy. They cover clean-ups for special situations. The first list itemizes what to do when unexpected company gives you only a short time to prepare.

Checklist for Monthly Projects

I do these on a day *other than* the thorough weekly cleaning day. I do one each week to keep from getting behind on these big jobs.
1st week: Clean oven and range
2nd week: Clean refrigerator and outside surfaces of cabinets
3rd week: Mop and wax kitchen floors and clean shower stall
4th week: Clean baseboards and ledges; wash scatter rugs, blankets, etc.
5th week: Clean any closets, cupboards, and drawers necessary
Note: Not all months have five "Wednesdays," or whatever day you choose. In that case, combine projects accordingly.

Checklist for Quarterly Projects

First month: polish furniture and repair scars. (Once a year, I remove old wax and apply new.)—See Cleaning Recipes #3 and #5
Second month: Sort seasonal clothing
Third month: Polish silver
Fourth month: Wash windows (A school-age child can wash his/her own bedroom windows)

"There's another special time—when we have to catch up in a hurry because we've gotten behind due to illness—our own or one of the youngsters—or there's been extended company, or whatever. That's where this next sheet will come in handy, I hope."

Renae turned to Betty, "Hey, 'Christian sister,' you might get called on more than you think!"

"'Christian sister,' yourself!" Betty grinned. "I like these practical ideas; I think they'll really work!"

Turning to the next sheet, Shirley went on, "In this connection, I've added some 'Tips to Make Cleaning Easier.' They're just some practical ideas that are not new or ex-

---

Checklist for Semi-Annual Projects

Clean draperies
Wash and iron curtains
Shampoo carpets
Clean walls
Rearrange furniture
Make any repairs necessary

Note: I find that if I attempt only one room at a time and spend from a day to a week on it (depending on its size), I can keep up with the meals, wash, and light routine cleaning of the rest of the house. The average house can be thoroughly cleaned this way over a month's time, twice a year.

The Ten-Minute Emergency Clean-Up

What to do when your old college roomie calls to say she's passing through town and will be over to see you in ten minutes . . .

1. Close the doors to any rooms you know won't be in use. (Be sure you have completed the "Six Imperatives for the Morning.")
2. Go through the rest of the rooms with a box or laundry basket, piling into it all out-of-place items.
3. Put any dirty dishes into the sink in scalding, soapy water to soak.
4. Wipe visible dirt from tables and floors with a rag or sponge.
5. In the bathroom(s), close shower curtain if tub is soiled. Wipe visible dirt from sinks or floor. Be sure guest towels are handy.
6. Carpet-sweep or vacuum where there is noticeable dirt on floor or carpet, especially in heavy traffic areas.
7. Dust table tops with a feather duster.

---

clusive to me, but it may help you to have them written down.

Catching Up When You're Behind

How not to be overwhelmed when you're sick, or have company all week, or just have a week of constant unexpected demands on your time . . .

1. Clean what is most important to you and your family. To me, it would be floors and bathrooms. To someone else, it might be clean clothes and a shining kitchen. Let the dust collect this week.
2. Prepare simple meals and do only essential laundry.
3. Don't feel guilty about getting off schedule or behind in your work. Just get back on where you left off and work gradually toward your normal routine.
4. Your cleaning schedule is your *servant* to help you accomplish your vision of your home; it is not your *master* to drive you.
5. Don't be too shy to ask your Christian sisters to help you out when you're really in a tight bind. Only pride keeps us from saying, "Help!"

Tips to Make Cleaning Easier

1. Clean as you go. Try to clean up a mess as soon as you make it. Try to leave a room as orderly as you found it—or more so.

2. Keep your cleaning supplies and equipment in workable condition. Always wash dust cloths, rags, mop and floor wax applicator immediately after use and return them to the Cleaning Caddy. Nothing is more exasperating than to be ready to clean and be out of clean rags or cleaning supplies or find the vacuum cleaner "on the blink."

3. Buy the best appliances you can afford. Buy what *you* need and will use.

   Good quality equipment is worth the investment in terms of good service and savings of your time and energy.

   I suggest you go to the library and read how *Consumer's Guide* rates the appliance you're interested in buying. Ask friends what problems they've had. To buy the best quality you can afford, wait for a sale.

"One of the things we all do together is work in the yard. The promise of a trip to the beach afterward or a cool "Icee" keeps us motivated.

"Many of us seem to forget that children can be invaluable as helpers. Some mothers I know say it takes more time to teach a child what to do and then supervise to see that the job is done properly than to do it herself. That may be, but when you train a child to do a job *properly*, you are teaching him a lifetime experience in discipline. You are gaining a helper and building his or her self-worth as a competent person.

"How many of us have heard—or said—that things aren't done as well as they used to be, people don't seem to care about doing things right, and so on? Much of it is because there was a generation of permissiveness, when children were not required to do anything they didn't want to. And we're all paying for it now. Children can be valuable helpers when they know what they are expected to do and how to do it.

"I thought you might be interested in the very first schedule that our son Todd made. He was seven and had seen me make schedules, so he made one for himself and hung it on his wall. I've kept it all these years. He had it in one long piece, five by twenty-two inches, but—to show you—I've cut it in half and put it together.

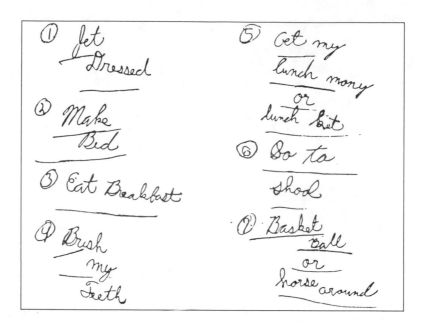

"The best way we have found to keep children motivated to do their chores is to have a family conference and together make a list of what needs to be done to make our home a glory to God. Then we distribute the tasks according to the age and ability of each child. Recognizing the ability of each child is important, since children vary in what they can accomplish at any age. But don't be afraid to give a child something a little beyond his or her abilities. Help them stretch! And don't be concerned about accepting gracefully a little-less-than-perfect performance.

"The children should know that the parents are also doing certain chores. In our home, we *all* take turns at the kitchen sink. Through the family conference, we found that the most-disliked chore was washing dishes. So we decided to help the children with this chore by taking a turn ourselves. The children in return took one of our chores, such as pulling the weeds in the flower beds each week.

"To motivate the children to do their best, we found the ideas on the next sheet to work well.

Motivating Children

1. Assign specific chores.
2. Teach the child how to do them well.
3. Set a definite day and time for a chore to be done, such as "Monday after school."
4. Post the list on the child's bedroom door or bulletin board for easy reference.

   (If one child feels his chores are unfair or that he would like to "change jobs," have a family conference.)

"Sometimes we mothers forget that even small children can do chores. Three-year-olds usually want to 'help' Mommie. We can use that time to teach preschoolers the basic how-to's of getting dressed, putting away pajamas, brushing or combing hair, helping to make their bed (and probably everyone else's too!), folding washcloths and rolling socks. Incidentally, I found that a good way to teach colors to my Debbie. A three-year-old can also help clear the table, empty wastebaskets, and pick up toys before bedtime. If these routines are established in the beginning, when the child wants to help, it is easier to carry them over into the times he *doesn't* want to.

"A young school-age child can do all of the above, with additions according to time, schoolwork, and outside activities. We must be careful that a child doesn't use one of those activities as a handy excuse to get out of assigned chores.

"Arrange things so that your children won't need you to take care of all their everyday needs. For example, even a four-year-old can pour herself a glass of milk if both glass and milk are within reach.

"You will find a sample chore sheet for a school-age child among your papers, and also a list of suggestions for other

---

Suggested Chores for Children

    For preschoolers (discretionary):
Set table
Feed pet (if it doesn't mean using a can opener)
Help clean and straighten closets and drawers
Empty dishwasher (may need help)

    For school children (discretionary):
Vacuum
Dust
Help put away groceries
Empty garbage
Sweep walks
Help in meal preparation
Wash windows, mirrors
Polish shoes
Wash car and clean inside
Mow the lawn
Make parts of meals, salads, desserts, etc.

---

chores your children might assume, depending on age and ability.

"For children who sometimes neglect or 'forget' to pick up dirty clothes or toys, you might want to have a 'Displaced Box.' It has worked wonders in ours and in other families.

"You probably know how the system works. To get an item back, the owner must perform some service or job for you. Be sure that whatever you require the child to do is roughly proportionate to the value of the item he or she

My Responsibilities

Sample Chore Sheet

Daily
1. Make bed before school
2. Set dinner table
3. Do dishes when my turn
4. Feed pet; clean up after pet
5. Keep room tidy; pick up clothes and toys before school and before bed-time

Weekly

Monday
6. Take out garbage before school
7. Sweep back porch after school
8. Put clean clothes away (Monday is wash day)

Tuesday
9. Pull weeds in backyard flower beds

Wednesday
10. Dust and vacuum my room

Thursday
11. Wash bathroom mirrors

Friday
No Chores Today

Saturday
12. Wash car

wants, the number of times reminders have to be given, and so on.

"Ephesians 6:3 has a good 'reminder' for us parents. As the New International Version puts it: '. . . do not exasperate your children; instead, bring them up in the training and instruction of the Lord.'"

15

Our Role Model

At various times during these six weeks, I've mentioned the 'excellent wife' described in Proverbs 31:10–31. Her worth is more than precious gems, 'far above jewels'! According to the passage, this woman takes such good care of her family in every aspect of their lives that her husband praises her, her children bless her, and her works bring her honor. I long to pattern my life after hers, don't you?

"Let's take a look at this model wife—her characteristics and how she handles her priorities. I've matched them up with the scriptural priorities we looked at in our first session."

THE EXCELLENT WIFE
Proverbs 31:10–31

Her Priorities

Toward God

She is a woman who fears and reverences the Lord (v. 30).

Toward Her Family

Her Husband

1. She is trustworthy
   "The heart of her husband trusts in her . . ." (v. 11a).
2. She richly satisfies his needs
   ". . . he will have no lack of gain" (v. 11b).
3. She helps him
   "She does him good . . ." (v. 12a).
4. She does not hinder him
   ". . . and not evil/All the days of her life" (v. 12b).

Her Children

1. She disciplines them
   "She watches over the affairs of her household . . ."
   (v. 27, NIV).
2. She feeds and clothes them well
   ". . . she provides food for her family . . ." (v. 15, NIV).
   They "are clothed with scarlet" (v. 21b).
3. She teaches them by word
   ". . . faithful instruction is on her tongue" (v. 26b, NIV).
4. She teaches them by example
   . . . to honor their father, her husband (vv. 11–12).
   . . . to work hard (vv. 17, 27).
   . . . to enjoy work (v. 13).
   . . . to be disciplined (vv. 15a, 18).
   . . . to plan ahead (vv. 21, 25).
   . . . to help others (v. 20).
   . . . to be financially free (vv. 16, 24).
   . . . to be what God has planned for them to be (v. 30).

Toward Her Homemaking

She is a "domestic engineer."

1. She "looks well to the ways of her household" (v. 27a).
2. She has a daily blueprint—"plans the day's work" (v. 15c, LB).
3. She rises early and works late (vv. 15a, 18b).
4. She is diligent—"looks for wool and flax . . . works with her hands . . . does not eat the bread of idleness" (vv. 13, 27b).
5. She enjoys her work—"works with her hands in delight" (v. 13b).
6. She is a good shopper—"brings her food from afar" (v. 14b).

She is financially wise.

1. She is prudent—"considers a field and buys it" (v. 16a).
2. She is a bargain-hunter—"watches for bargains" (v. 18a, LB).
3. She reinvests her earnings—"From her earnings she plants . . ." (v. 16b).

Toward Herself

1. She is a woman of "strength and dignity" (v. 25a).
2. She "has no fear of old age" (v. 25b, LB).
3. She is discreet—"opens her mouth in wisdom . . ." (v. 26a).
4. She is realistic and aware she is doing a good job, "senses that her gain is good . . ." (v. 18a).
5. She looks her best—her clothing is "beautifully made" (v. 22b, LB).

Toward Others

1. She is energetic and "girds herself with strength . . ." (v. 17).
2. She is generous to the needy—"She sews for the poor, and generously gives to the needy" (v. 20, LB).

3. She is a businesswoman—"She makes linen garments and sells them and supplies the merchants with sashes" (v. 24, NIV).
4. She is a credit to her husband—"her husband is respected at the city gate, where he takes his seat among the elders of the land" (v. 23, NIV).
5. She is wise and kind (v. 26).

The Results
1. She is not afraid of the future; she has made provision (v. 21).
2. Her husband is well-known, with a good reputation (v. 23).
3. She is praised (as a result of doing all she was supposed to do!)
   • by her children and her husband (v. 28).
   • by her works, because what she does she does well (v. 31).

"GIVE HER THE REWARD SHE HAS EARNED, AND LET HER WORKS BRING HER PRAISE AT THE CITY GATE" (v. 31, NIV).

"What a wonderful woman! What great rewards she earns! What bountiful results she reaps!—and it all comes about because she has her priorities right: she fears and reverences God.

"It is exciting for me to consider what God will bring into my life as I trust his wisdom and sovereignty. The delightful people I will meet. The freedom from fretting, tension, and stress. The positive attitude I will have toward circumstances that I know are in his control. The provisions he will make for my needs. God, my heavenly Father, is totally responsible for me!

"Isn't it wonderful to think that he treats us all alike! And what he has promised to do for me, he has promised to do for *you*, if you will trust him. Ladies, I'm excited, and I'm encouraged, when I consider what wonderfully amazing things

God wants to do with us and our husbands and children and our homes.

"Will you join me in praying?"

Father, as we think about ourselves, about our homes and the relationships there, our prayer is that you might be honored and glorified. We pray that we will look to you as the One who will point out our priorities and show us our vital part as the women in our homes.

Father, we thank you for what you are doing in our hearts as you remind us that what takes place within the family unit is as important—no, is *more* important—than clean walls and scrubbed floors. Help us to keep both in proper perspective—*your* perspective. Thank you. Amen.

16

Renae: Managing to Be Free

Renac stared blankly at her hand, still on the phone. *Perhaps,* she thought, *if I simply do nothing, if there is no sound, no motion, no thought, then nothing will have happened.*

It would still be Friday morning. She would be in the kitchen, and her thoughts would be returning to Shirley's prayer at the end of the seminar. She loved the part where they had prayed together for "God's perspective" on their homes, relationships, and "clean walls and scrubbed floors." She knew just where she was going to hang the framed "Beatitudes of a Christian Wife" she had purchased at the end of the last class.

Out the window this morning the tall grass in the meadow behind the house had ruffled in the summer breeze that blew in from the river. Fluffy white clouds, holding out a promise of rain but probably not going to deliver, shadowed the grass.

Now a full moon loomed bleakly in the night sky. Still not moving, frozen in time, Renae saw herself smiling as she finished her "Six Imperatives" that morning. What Shirley had said was so true: carrying out the house-cleaning schedule wasn't nearly as much work as worrying about it had been!

And Steve was as pleased as she herself, with the clean, well-organized home that was emerging from the mess. Even now, hours later, Renae felt her face warming as she remembered his extravagant compliments. Incongruously, she recalled putting away the dishwater soap under the sink and looking around at the sparkling counters earlier that day.

Even the girls seemed to find things more attractive. The girls! She moaned softly as she thought of her daughters, then deliberately turned her mind back to the morning.

She remembered trying to picture that "excellent wife" from Proverbs, doing the sort of thing that women all over the world spend their time doing: shopping, cooking, sewing, gardening, washing, cleaning, entertaining and being entertained by a few close friends.

She was working at memorizing those verses, but all she could remember was the phrase, "She smiles at the future. . . ." She remembered thinking, *That's what I'm doing! Now that I am learning God's perspective, I'm smiling at the future!*

But that was before the phone had rung! Renae stared at her hand, unmoving on the receiver she had replaced in its cradle. She was vaguely aware of the ticking of the clock, but it seemed that time had stopped. Then Steve was pulling at her arm, almost shouting, "What? Renae, tell me what!"

She and Steve had not begun worrying about the girls until 9:30 that night. "I suppose they might have gone somewhere for ice cream after the early movie," Steve had said.

"Something's wrong," Renae had answered, shaking her head. "They're always home on time—or call to let us know they'll be late."

At 10:30 Steve had snapped off the TV with an exasperated invective. He alternately paced the living room and peered out at the empty street. Renae had tried to knit but gave up when she couldn't concentrate on the pattern. Finally, they had just waited in silence.

It was 11:45 when the ringing telephone made them both jump. Renae flew to answer it. *Kathy!* she thought.

Instead it was the hospital, with a grim message.

Very carefully Renae replaced the receiver in its cradle. Her hand stayed there, unmoving. She opened her mouth, but no words came out.

Then Steve shook her, shouting again, "Renae! Snap out of it! What happened?"

Her voice wavered on the edge of a sob, repeating words her mind still refused to accept.

"An accident—a crosswalk—a speeding driver— didn't stop—Kathy okay—but Melissa—"

There was a rush and a flurry then. A frantic ride through a montage of changing lights, darkened buildings, empty streets. There in the car, Renae felt a chill, beginning at the core of her being. She had prayed over and over, "Let Missy be okay. Give me strength to go through this. Please let Missy be okay."

Now, with nails biting into her palms, Renae stared out the wide hospital window into the murky darkness. Here and there, headlights flashed as cars moved in or out of the parking lot. It had been hours since that phone call. *Would the night never end? Would Missy—?*

She was weary from worry, her eyes scratchy from lack of sleep and anguished tears. She glanced at her watch: 5:30 A.M.

"God—" she started to pray, then stopped, not knowing what to say, filled with dark, hollow pain.

Hours ago now, Kathy—shaken and bruised but all right, thank God!—had gone home with Steve. The thought of her elder daughter brought a fleeting smile to Renae's lips. With teenage determination, Kathy had scowled, furiously blink-

ing back the tears, and refused to leave Melissa. Steve had
finally convinced her, promising, "I'll bring you back to see
your sister. By morning she should be conscious."

Kathy had looked at him soberly; then she nodded and
walked with her parents to the door of the hospital room.
There Steve had turned to Renae with a private smile of great
tenderness, and she had buried her face against his shoulder.
He had held her tightly a moment, then gently lifted her face
toward his.

"Renae, I love you," he had said, moving his lips slowly
against hers. "I hate to leave you, darling, but—"

He had cleared his throat then and tried to smile again as
they looked toward Melissa's bed. "Call me if there's any
change." Steve bent to kiss her cheek again and was gone.

In the stillness of the hospital, among the hushed but busy
nurses, Renae made a conscious effort to unclench her
hands. Drooping with grief and fatigue, she slumped against
the window ledge. *What was there about a hospital,* she
wondered, *that made you feel so inadequate, so helpless, so
alone and lonely?*

"God, I'm glad you're here," she whispered.

Her face white and weary, Renae closed her eyes briefly
and wished she could erase the whole night. But the oxygen
unit hissed behind her, an audible evidence of reality.

Melissa moaned, tried to turn. Renae walked back to the
bed and touched her hand, but there was no answering pres-
sure. *How very small she looked beneath the white sheet!*
Her straight brown hair spilled lankly over the pillow, half
hiding the bandage on her forehead. There were ominous
tubes bearing mysterious fluids into and away from her body.
Her right leg was in a cast and one hand was swathed in
bandages. Her skin was a dull grayish color.

"She's going to be all right. The doctor *said* so," Renae
told herself, one hand tightly covering her mouth. She was
shaken again by a wave of the fear and anxiety that had not
left her since she had understood what the voice on the
telephone was saying.

Renae took a deep steadying breath. Gently she caressed the fingers of Melissa's uninjured hand, singing softly the songs that had quieted her as a baby.

Then she prayed: "Listen, Lord, please listen—I don't understand this accident. I don't understand anything about why Melissa and Kathy have to suffer the shock and pain. But I thank you that they're going to be—" Suddenly she was sobbing. "—all right. I told you the other night, Father, that I was giving all my family to you, but—"

She grabbed a tissue from the night table and mopped her face.

"I remember Shirley prayed—was it only yesterday, Lord?—that you might be honored and glorified in our lives. And that's what I want. I really do.

"And, oh! God, I'm glad I went to that seminar; not just for what I learned about schedules and priorities and how to keep house. But mostly because the best thing for me was to get to know you, to find out that you love me—and my family—that you have a plan for my life. Thank you for being here right now, in this hospital room with us. With Melissa and me.

"I'm so glad you're here. Touch Melissa, Lord, please touch her—"

Renae leaned wearily against the bed, Melissa's hand still clasped in hers. Her eyes searched the pale, still face.

The rising sun sent orange-pink rays over the quiet streets with their charming homes set on groomed lawns. Palm fronds and orange trees stirred, waking lazily in the morning breeze from the river.

The oxygen unit hissed. Melissa's eyes opened, focused on her mother's face, and closed peacefully again.

Appendix A
Have You Heard the Good News?

In a world filled with bad news, we are offered the good news of a marvelous gift!

You cannot earn it, or buy it, or be good enough to deserve it. To receive it, you must know you need it and must want it more than anything else. It is a wonderful gift. And it is a gift no one but God can give you.

Just as the night sky sharpens the brightness of the stars, and the pain of childbirth underlines a mother's joy when she sees her newborn babe, so the darkness of bad times emphasizes the brilliance of glad tidings. To fully understand God's Good News, you must know about the bad news, too.

Why Do You Need the Good News?

There are three reasons we need this Good News.

Reason #1: God's character

What kind of God do you think God is? Most people have an opinion, but their opinion is not necessarily the truth. The Bible is God's Word, telling us what he is like, and, he declares, ". . . I the LORD your God am holy" (Lev. 19:2).

The apostle John says, "And this is the message we have heard from Him and announce to you, that God is light, and in Him there is no darkness [evil] at all" (1 John 1:5). God is holy. He has no evil in his character. He cannot be stained by evil. He cannot excuse evil.

Reason #2: God's character sets the standard for man

God created man to be like himself in character and conduct: "And God created man in His own image, in the image of God He created him; male and female He created them" (Gen. 1:27).

God planned for you to be the visible expression of what he, the invisible God, is like. That is God's purpose for your life.

In other words, if God were a human being, what kind of life would he live? He tells us in Exodus 20:1–17:

"You shall have no other gods before Me" (v. 3).

"You shall not make for yourself an idol . . ." (v. 4).

"You shall not take the name of the LORD your God in vain . . ." (v. 7).

"Remember the sabbath day, to keep it holy" (v. 8).

"Honor your father and your mother . . ." (v. 12).

"You shall not murder" (v. 13).

"You shall not commit adultery" (v. 14).

"You shall not steal" (v. 15).

"You shall not bear false witness against your neighbor" (v. 16).

"You shall not covet . . ." (v. 17).

This is the standard of quality for God's kind of man and woman. It is his requirement for both your outward conduct and your inner thoughts and desires every day of your life.

Reason #3. You have failed to meet God's standard

God is the judge of whether we fulfill his requirements for a holy and righteous life. Our good opinion of ourselves does not carry any weight with him. He who knows all things says, "There is none righteous, not even one . . . there is none who does good, there is not even one. . . . for all have sinned and fall short of the glory of God" (Rom. 3:10–12, 23).

Your disobedience to God's law is called sin. ". . . sin is lawlessness" (1 John 3:4). Sin offends Holy God.

The Judge's verdict? Guilty!

The sentence? Death! Eternal punishment and separation from God. "For the wages of sin is death . . ." (Rom. 6:23). "And these [the unrighteous] will go away into eternal punishment . . ." (Matt. 25:46).

You need good news because of the bad news that your failure before God puts you in danger of eternal punishment in hell.

What Is The Good News?

Because of his love, God provided his one and only Son, Jesus Christ, to take the punishment *you* deserve for not measuring up to God's standard.

Jesus Christ lived a righteous life. He never failed to obey God's laws. He then willingly gave himself to die on a cross for your sins. He suffered God's wrath for you. He now offers you the record of his perfect life as a free gift.

The Bible says, "For Christ also died for sins once for all, the just for the unjust, in order that He might bring us to God . . ." (1 Peter 3:18). "He [God] made Him [Jesus Christ] who knew no sin to be sin on our behalf, that we might become the righteousness of God in Him" (2 Cor. 5:21).

Christ died for your sins. He offers you his righteousness.

An amazing event followed Jesus' death. Three days later, Jesus "was declared the Son of God with power *by the resurrection from the dead . . .*" (Rom. 1:4, italics added). Death was defeated!

We know that "God has made Him both Lord and Christ . . ." (Acts 2:36). As Lord, the Son of God has authority to give eternal life in heaven to those who receive the Good News.

Will You Receive the Good News?

Adam, the first man, rebelled against God by disobeying the Creator's specific command not to eat the fruit of the tree of the knowledge of good and evil. This disobedience severed his relationship with God. It brought him and all his descendants—the whole human race—into a broken relationship with God and a state of sin (Rom. 5:12).

Because we are born from Adam, we are born severed from God and are his "enemies." In addition, the whole human race followed in Adam's steps of disobedience. We have chosen to please ourselves rather than to obey God.

Because of God's own holiness and justice, he *must* judge man's disobedience, or sin. Yet, in love and mercy, God has provided a way out for those who will receive his gracious gift.

The Bible makes this clear: "He who believes in the Son has eternal life; but he who does not obey the Son shall not see life, but the wrath of God abides on him" (John 3:36).

We either believe and obey his Son, or we receive his wrath—eternal punishment.

What Must I Do?

Are you asking what you must do to receive this gift? The Bible says, "Repent, and let each of you be baptized in the name of Jesus Christ for the forgiveness of your sins; and you shall receive the gift of the Holy Spirit" (Acts 2:38).

The Holy Spirit is the essence of the resurrected and living Christ, coming to live within you to empower you to live a new life. Will you accept the Savior and commit your life in obedience to God's will?

To trust in someone means to count on a person to do exactly what he promised. It means you have confidence that he is able to do what he promised. Will you trust the Lord Jesus Christ as your only means to be right with God? Right now?

If so, sign and date this pledge, to commemorate this wonderful day!

The Way of Salvation

Today I receive the Good News.

I trust Jesus Christ to be my Lord and Savior—my only means to be right with God.

I commit my life to follow him daily in obedience.

Signed _____

Date _____

Appendix B: Work Sheets

My Present Schedule

TIME	SUNDAY	MONDAY	TUESDAY	WEDNESDAY	THURSDAY	FRIDAY	SATURDAY
6:00							
7:00							
8:00							
9:00							
10:00							
11:00							
12:00							
1:00							
2:00							

3:00	4:00	5:00	6:00	7:00	8:00	9:00	10:00	11:00	Additional Things To Do

My Present Schedule

TIME	SUNDAY	MONDAY	TUESDAY	WEDNESDAY	THURSDAY	FRIDAY	SATURDAY
6:00							
7:00							
8:00							
9:00							
10:00							
11:00							
12:00							
1:00							
2:00							

3:00	**4:00**	**5:00**	**6:00**	**7:00**	**8:00**	**9:00**	**10:00**	**11:00**	**Additional Things To Do**

My Life Purpose: What I Hope to Be

_____

_____

_____

_____

_____

_____

_____

My Priorities

1. _____

_____

2. _____

_____

3. _____

_____

4. _____

_____

5. _____

_____

_____